Southern Living

ideas for great

KITCHENS

Oxmoor House®

Southern Living® Ideas for Great Kitchens was adapted from a book by the same title published by Sunset Books.

Staff for this book:

developmental editor:
Linda J. Selden

book editor:
Scott Atkinson

consulting editor:
Jane Horn

editorial coordinator:
Vicki Weathers

copy editor:
Marcia Williamson

design:
Barbara Vick

computer production:
Linda Bouchard

illustrations:
Mark Pechenik

principal photographer:
Philip Harvey

photo director:
JoAnn Masaoka Van Atta

production coordinator:
Patricia S. Williams

Our appreciation to the staff of Southern Living® magazine for their contributions to this book.

First printing January 2000
Copyright © 2000 by Oxmoor House, Inc.
Book Division of Southern Progress Corporation
P.O. Box 2463
Birmingham, Alabama 35201

ISBN 0-376-09076-6
Library of Congress Catalog Card Number: 99-65015

Printed in the United States
Cover design by James Boone and Vasken Guiragossian. Photography by Emily Minton, Southern Progress Photo Collection.

A perfect recipe

Cook up the kitchen of your dreams with this newly revised title as your guide. You'll find the latest in beautiful, efficient designs and materials. From a comfortable armchair, you can examine scores of up-to-the-minute kitchen styles in full color. Or explore the possibilities in European cabinetry, convection ovens, residential/commercial ranges, and low-voltage light fixtures. If you're ready to dig in, you'll also find a solid introduction to kitchen planning as practiced by the pros.

Many kitchen professionals and homeowners provided information and encouragement or let us take a look at their new creations. We'd especially like to thank The Plumbery and The Kitchen Source at The Bath & Beyond. Our thanks also go to Chugrad McAndrews who spent many hours ably assisting with location photography.

Design credits for specific photos are listed on pages 110–111.

contents

what's cooking?

E FFICIENCY, flexibility, and a bit of fun—that's the recipe for today's kitchen. More varied than ever, kitchen design features sophisticated new colors, fresh styles, and innovative components.

Many homeowners appreciate the clean lines and bright colors of the European-style kitchen. Its frameless cabinets, in high-gloss lacquer or laminate, hold a score of efficient aids such as lazy Susans, wire-frame pullouts, and built-in pantry packs. Appliances are built in, from the refrigerator and microwave oven to the toaster. Gleaming gourmet accessories abound. Even sinks and faucets debut in new shapes and finishes.

On the other hand, cheery country and traditional styles are on the rebound. Often the focus of a kitchen is its freestanding range, either a high-output "residential/commercial" model or a reconditioned heirloom. Adding warmth and hospitality are homey accents like pot racks, freestanding furniture, open shelving or plate rails, tiled backsplashes, and hardwood flooring.

In many families, the kitchen is evolving into an all-purpose room, including dining table or breakfast booth, computer desk, entertainment area, fireplace—even laundry center. Popular as ever are kitchen islands and peninsulas, which define the work area yet allow the cook to converse freely with family and friends.

A PLANNING PRIMER

Sit back, close your eyes, and visualize your dream kitchen. Do sleek new cabinets and gleaming appliances float before your eyes? Now come back down to earth. What's the clearance between the dishwasher and that new granite-topped island? If you're not quite sure how to fit the pieces together, this book will help. USE THIS CHAPTER as a workbook, a sequential course in basic kitchen planning. Begin by evaluating your existing kitchen; wind your way through layout and design basics; then meet the professionals who can give you a hand. FOR IDEAS and inspiration, peruse the color photos in the next two chapters, examining the many views of successful design solutions and getting familiar with the latest in cooktops, downlights, and built-ins. That dream kitchen will reappear, this time on solid ground.

taking stock

FIRST THINGS FIRST. *Before you rush into a shopping spree, take the time to survey what you have now. A clear, accurate base map is your most useful planning tool.*

Measure the space

To make your kitchen survey, you'll need either a folding wooden rule (shown above) or steel measuring tape. First, sketch out your present layout (don't worry about scale), doodling in windows, doors, islands, and other features. Then measure the elements along each wall at counter height.

After you finish measuring one wall, total the figures; then take an overall measurement from corner to corner. The two figures should match, Measure the height of each wall in the same manner.

Make a base map

Now draw your kitchen to scale on graph paper—most kitchen designers use ½-inch scale (¼₂ actual size). An architect's scale is helpful but isn't really required. Some standard drafting paper with ¼-inch squares and a T square and triangle greatly simplify matters.

The example shown below includes both centerlines to the sink plumbing and electrical symbols—outlets, switches, and fixtures. Add any other features that may affect your plans.

A SAMPLE BASE MAP

ARCHITECTURAL SYMBOLS

WALL

WINDOW

DOOR SWING

DUPLEX WALL OUTLET

WALL SWITCH
CEILING FIXTURE

WALL FIXTURE

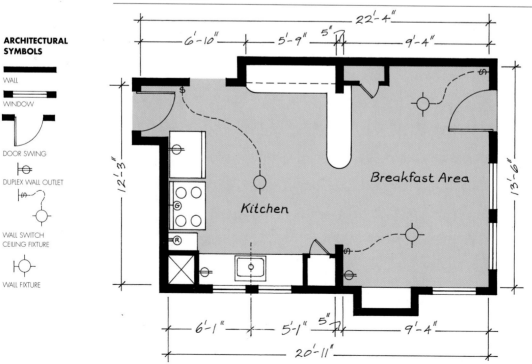

22'-4"

6'-10"   5'-9"   5"   9'-4"

12'-3"

13'-6"

Kitchen

Breakfast Area

6'-1"   5'-1"   5"   9'-4"

20'-11"

A Kitchen Questionnaire

This questionnaire will organize your responses to your present kitchen and stimulate your thoughts about exactly what you want in a new one. When used along with your base map, it also provides a starting point for discussing your ideas with architects, designers, or showroom personnel. Note your answers on a separate sheet of paper, adding any important preferences or dislikes. Then gather your notes, any clippings you've collected, and a copy of your base map, and you're ready to begin.

1. What's your main reason for changing your kitchen?

2. How many are in your household? List adults, teens, children, seniors, pets.

3. Will this be a two-cook kitchen?

4. Are users right-handed? Left-handed? How tall?

5. Is the kitchen to be used by a disabled person? Is that person confined to a wheelchair?

6. Do you entertain frequently? Formally? Informally? Do you like compartmentalized work spaces or great-room (open) designs?

7. Would you like an island or peninsula?

8. What secondary activity areas do you want?
   ☐ Baking center ☐ Planning desk or office
   ☐ Breakfast nook ☐ Entertainment center
   ☐ Laundry/ironing center ☐ Wet bar

9. Are you considering any structural modifications?
   ☐ Skylight ☐ Greenhouse window or sunroom
   ☐ Second cook's alcove ☐ Pass-through ☐ Other

10. Is the kitchen located on the first or second floor? Is there a full basement, crawl space, or concrete slab below? Is there a second floor, attic, or open ceiling above?

11. Can present doors and windows be moved? Could an interior wall be removed to enlarge the kitchen? Is an addition possible?

12. Can existing plumbing be moved? To where?

13. What type of heating system do you have? Do any walls contain ducting?

14. What's the rating of your electrical service?

15. What flooring do you have? Do you need new flooring? ☐ Wood ☐ Resilient ☐ Ceramic tile
   ☐ Stone ☐ Other

16. What are present wall and ceiling coverings? What wall treatments do you like? ☐ Paint ☐ Wallpaper
   ☐ Wood ☐ Tile ☐ Faux finish ☐ Plaster ☐ Glass block

17. List your present appliances. What new appliances are you planning? Will they be built in or freestanding?

18. What overall style (for example, high-tech, country, or regional) do you have in mind for your kitchen?

19. What style is your home's exterior? What style are adjacent interior spaces?

20. What color schemes do you prefer?

21. What storage needs do you have? What items do you use daily? Weekly? Monthly? What don't you need? What will you add in the future?

22. What are your cabinet requirements?
   ☐ Appliance garage ☐ Pullout shelves
   ☐ Lazy Susan ☐ Tilt-down sink front ☐ Pantry pack
   ☐ Storage wall with pullout bins ☐ Tray divider
   ☐ Drying rack ☐ Spice storage ☐ Flatware drawer
   ☐ Pullout cutting board ☐ Knife storage
   ☐ Wine rack ☐ Waste container ☐ Recycling bins
   ☐ Open shelving ☐ Other

23. Which cabinet materials do you like—wood, laminate, or other? If wood, should it be painted or stained? Light or dark? If natural, do you want oak, maple, pine, cherry? Do you want flat, raised, or recessed panel doors? Glass doors on wall cabinets?

24. Should the soffit space above wall cabinets be boxed in? Open for decorative articles? Or should cabinets run continuous to the ceiling?

25. What countertop materials do you prefer?
   ☐ Laminate ☐ Ceramic tile ☐ Solid-surface
   ☐ Wood ☐ Stone ☐ Stainless steel
   More than one material?

26. Do you want a 4-inch or full backsplash? Should it match or contrast with countertops?

27. Would you prefer a vent hood or downdraft stovetop ventilation system? Do you want a decorative ceiling fan?

28. What lighting type or types would work best?
   ☐ Incandescent ☐ Fluorescent ☐ Halogen
   ☐ 120-volt or low-voltage?

29. What fixture types will you need?
   ☐ Surface-mounted ☐ Recessed downlights
   ☐ Track lights ☐ Pendant fixtures
   ☐ Undercabinet strips ☐ Indirect soffit lighting
   ☐ Display lights inside cabinets

30. What time framework do you have for completion?

31. What budget figure do you have in mind?

layout basics

NOW COMES *the fun of really planning your new kitchen. Layout is a three-part process that includes weighing basic options; blocking out storage, countertops, and work centers; and double-checking efficient heights and clearances. There's no perfect sequence—the trick is to work back and forth. In very small or oddly shaped spaces you'll certainly need to compromise.*

Classic kitchen layouts

While brainstorming, it helps to have some basic layout schemes in mind. The floor plans shown below are practical both for utilizing space well and for employing efficient work triangles (see facing page).

ONE-WALL KITCHEN. Small or open kitchens frequently make use of the one-wall design, incorporating a single line of cabinets and appliances. This is not ideal, as there is a lot of moving back and forth—from refrigerator to range to sink. Still, it's the only choice for some small areas or open floor plans.

CORRIDOR KITCHEN. A kitchen open at both ends is a candidate for the corridor or galley kitchen; the design works well as long as the distance between opposite walls is not too great. Traffic flow can be a problem—it's tough to divert kitchen cruisers away from the cook.

L-SHAPED KITCHEN. This layout utilizes two adjacent walls, spreading out the work centers; typically, the refrigerator is at one end, range or wall ovens are at the other end, and the sink is in the center. The L-shaped kitchen gives a comfortable work triangle. You'll have to decide how to utilize the corner space (see page 15).

SAMPLE LAYOUTS & WORK TRIANGLES

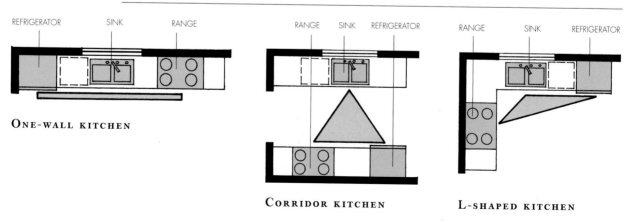

ONE-WALL KITCHEN

CORRIDOR KITCHEN

L-SHAPED KITCHEN

CONSIDER THE WORK TRIANGLE

Ever since kitchen layout studies in the 1950s introduced the term, designers have been evaluating kitchen efficiency by means of the work triangle. The three legs of the triangle connect the refrigerator, sink, and range (or cooktop). An efficient work triangle reduces the steps a cook must take during meal preparation. The ideal sum of the three legs is 26 feet or less, with individual legs no shorter than 4 feet and no longer than 9 feet. Whenever possible, the work triangle should be uninvaded by traffic flow.

Today, the reign of the work triangle is being challenged by two-cook layouts, elaborate island and peninsula work centers, and specialized appliances such as modular cooktops, built-in grills, and microwave and convection ovens. Nevertheless, the triangle is still a valuable starting point for planning kitchen efficiency. It may be useful to sketch in multiple triangles to cover different requirements.

U-SHAPED KITCHEN. Three adjacent walls make up the efficient U-shaped design (efficient, that is, as long as there is sufficient distance between opposite walls). Often this layout opens up space for auxiliary work areas in addition to the central work triangle—for example, a second sink for washing vegetables, a baking center, a second cooktop and dishwasher, or even a complete work center for a second cook.

G-SHAPED KITCHEN. This newly popular shape combines the efficient U-shaped layout with an attached peninsula at one end. The G shape offers plenty of opportunities for specialized work centers and helps shield the cook from distracting traffic; however, it may seem a little claustrophobic to some cooks.

WHAT ABOUT AN ISLAND? A kitchen island is a popular addition to many kitchen remodels. The extra cabinets and countertop add storage and work space, block off unwanted traffic flow, and can function as an eating counter.

On the minus side, islands can cramp space and cut into work triangles and traffic flows. And it's usually easier to bring utilities to a "landlocked" peninsula than to a free-floating island.

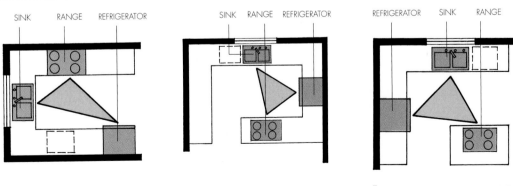

U-SHAPED KITCHEN   **G-SHAPED KITCHEN**   **L-SHAPED WITH ISLAND**

KITCHEN PLANNING AT A GLANCE

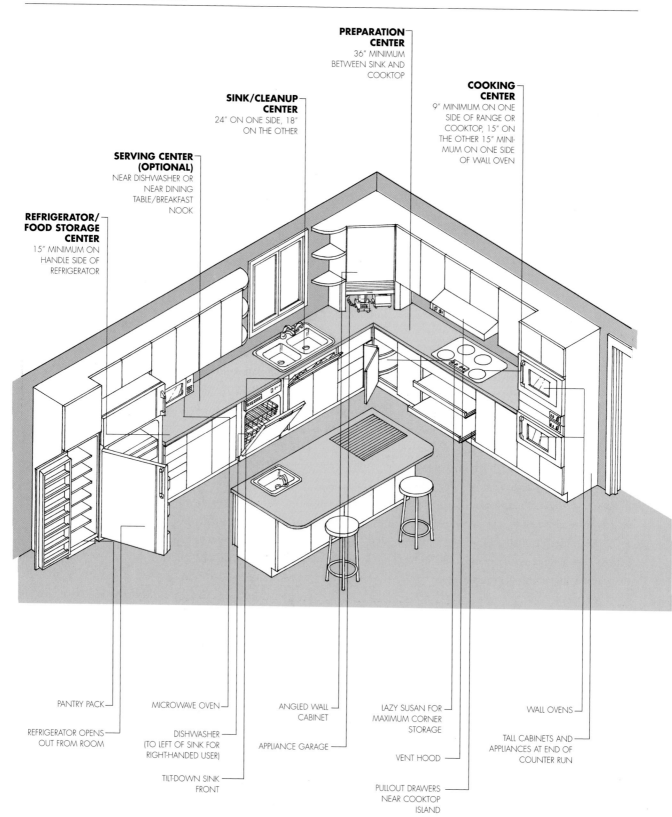

**PREPARATION
CENTER**
36" MINIMUM
BETWEEN SINK AND
COOKTOP

**SINK/CLEANUP
CENTER**
24" ON ONE SIDE, 18"
ON THE OTHER

**COOKING
CENTER**
9" MINIMUM ON ONE
SIDE OF RANGE OR
COOKTOP, 15" ON
THE OTHER 15" MINI-
MUM ON ONE SIDE
OF WALL OVEN

**SERVING CENTER
(OPTIONAL)**
NEAR DISHWASHER OR
NEAR DINING
TABLE/BREAKFAST
NOOK

**REFRIGERATOR/
FOOD STORAGE
CENTER**
15" MINIMUM ON
HANDLE SIDE OF
REFRIGERATOR

PANTRY PACK

REFRIGERATOR OPENS
OUT FROM ROOM

MICROWAVE OVEN

DISHWASHER
(TO LEFT OF SINK FOR
RIGHT-HANDED USER)

TILT-DOWN SINK
FRONT

ANGLED WALL
CABINET

APPLIANCE GARAGE

LAZY SUSAN FOR
MAXIMUM CORNER
STORAGE

VENT HOOD

PULLOUT DRAWERS
NEAR COOKTOP
ISLAND

WALL OVENS

TALL CABINETS AND
APPLIANCES AT END OF
COUNTER RUN

Mapping the work centers

One key to planning an efficient kitchen layout is to concentrate on the work centers, allowing for both adequate countertop space and storage in each area.

The drawing on the facing page outlines the major points you'll need to consider. The National Kitchen & Bath Association compiled these figures by studying many efficient kitchens, big and small; you may or may not be able to fit in all these features.

When plotting the centers, think through the steps you'd take bringing food into the house, preparing it, serving it, cleaning up, and storing plates and utensils. As a rule, items should be stored in the area of first use. The one exception? Everyday dishes and flatware: you might store them near the point of last use—the dishwasher or sink.

To sketch your evolving ideas, lay tracing paper on top of your new base map. You might make scale outlines of cabinet and appliance shapes, photocopy them, and cut them out. Move the cutouts around on a tracing of your base map, then draw the shapes onto the plan.

Refrigerator/food storage center. Allow at least 15 inches of countertop space on the handle side of the refrigerator as a landing area for groceries; if that's impossible, locate this space across from the fridge, no more than 48 inches away. Ideally, the refrigerator is at the end of a cabinet run, near an access door, with the door rotating out. (Need to place the refrigerator inside a cabinet run? Think about a built-in, side-by-side model, or one or more undercounter pullouts, as shown on pages 100–101.)

Also consider an 18- or 21-inch drawer unit. A smaller unit is too narrow to be useful, and drawers 24 inches or larger almost inevitably fill up with junk.

An over-the-refrigerator cabinet is a good storage place for infrequently used items. Custom pullouts or a stock "pantry pack" are an excellent use for the tall, narrow space beside the refrigerator.

Sink/cleanup center. More time is spent at the sink than anywhere else in the kitchen. So a main sink should be central in your plan, ideally at the center of the cook's work path. It's best to locate the sink and cleanup center between the refrigerator and range or cooktop.

Allow at least 24 inches of counter space on one side of the primary sink and 18 inches on the other. If you're planning a second, smaller sink elsewhere, those clearances can be less—3 inches and 18 inches. (In a corner, these figures may be the sum of two angled countertops.)

Traditionally, designers place the dishwasher for a right-hander to the left of the sink area and to the right for a lefty. But do whatever makes you comfortable. Either way, it should be placed within 36 inches of the sink's edge.

Plan to store cleaning supplies in or near the sink area. Many kinds of bins and pullouts—both built-ins and retrofits—are available for under-sink storage. Tilt-down fronts for sponges and other supplies are available on many sink base cabinets. This is also a prime location for waste and recycling bins; again, pullout and tilt-down options abound.

Preparation center. It's ideal to locate this center adjacent to a sink and between the sink and cooktop or range. Alternatively, put it opposite the refrigerator on an island or peninsula supplied with a secondary sink and a cooktop.

Plan a minimum of 36 inches of countertop. If two centers are adjacent, add 12 inches to the longest countertop requirement. If two cooks work together, plan a minimum of 36 inches of counter space for each. A second sink can help the second cook immensely.

Although it may not be a good idea to raise and lower countertop heights (if you have an eye toward resale, that is), the preparation center is a good place to customize. A marble counter insert is a boon for the serious pastry chef.

Appliance garages with tambour or paneled doors are still popular for this area, but be sure to leave at least 16 inches of usable counter depth outside such a cupboard. Need a place for

UNIVERSAL DESIGN

If you are remodeling to accommodate a disabled or elderly person, or if you're simply looking down the road, be aware of the growing trend toward universal or barrier-free design. In many cases, general recommendations for kitchen heights and clearances (see facing page) now reflect universal guidelines; but in addition, it's best to consider some specifics.

For example, does the kitchen have a low counter for sitting to chop vegetables or to cut out cookies? Is there a stool to pull up by the range for stirring food? Are doorways wide enough for a wheelchair? Is the eating area set up for easy access? What about the sink?

Special heights, clearances, and room dimensions may be required. To accommodate a wheelchair, the room's access door must be at least 32 inches wide and traffic patterns 36 inches wide. You'll also need to plan open turnaround areas near the sink and major appliances that are at least 30 by 48 inches.

It's important to leave the spaces below both sink and preparation areas open for seated use. The knee space should be a minimum of 30 inches wide by 27 inches high by 19 inches deep. Plan to enclose plumbing and gas and electric lines, but leave an access door.

Frequently used storage areas should be located between 15 and 48 inches high. Likewise, place door handles, switches, and other controls no higher than 48 inches from the floor.

You should also exchange standard door knobs, faucet handles, and cabinet hardware for levers and pulls that can be operated with one closed hand or a wrist.

Think comfort and safety. Allow extra task lighting for aging users, and strive to provide as many visual aids as possible—such as contrasting countertops and switches, and large, easy-to-read range or cooktop controls placed at the front of appliances. Aim for matte finishes, not glaring, glossy surfaces. Flooring should be slip resistant—carpeting is gaining in popularity. A batch-feed (lid-controlled) garbage disposal is safer than one controlled by a wall switch. Side-by-side refrigerators and side-hinged ovens are simpler to access. Consider electric heat sources instead of open gas flames. Some cooktops have automatic-shutoff features.

Also be on the lookout for the growing number of controls, fixtures, and fittings specifically designed for "universal" use.

spices or staples? An open shelf or backsplash rack will do the job. Knife drawers, pullout cutting boards, and waste or compost bins are other niceties to consider here.

COOKING CENTER. Plan at least 9 inches of countertop area on one side of the range or cooktop and 15 inches on the other as a landing area for hot pans and casseroles, and to allow pot handles to be turned to the side (for safety's sake) while pots are in use. If the range or cooktop meets a tall end cabinet, keep 15 inches on the open side and at least 3 inches on the cabinet side. Protect the cabinet with flame-retardant material.

You should also allow 15 inches of countertop beside a wall oven. If the oven does not open into a major traffic area, the 15 inches can be opposite, but no more than 48 inches away. Typically, wall ovens are placed at the end of a cabinet run. As separate wall ovens are used less frequently than the cooktop or range, they're considered outside the primary work triangle.

Although we think of the microwave oven as part of the cooking center, many people prefer to place it near the refrigerator/freezer or in a separate center. Mount the microwave so its bottom is from 24 to 48 inches off the floor. Again, plan to have at least one 15-inch landing zone nearby.

Plan to store frequently used pots and pans in base pullout drawers mounted on heavy-duty, full-extension drawer guides (see page 81). Frequently used utensils should be kept at least 22 inches off the floor.

SERVING CENTER. Everyday dishes, glassware, flatware, serving plates, and bowls, as well as napkins and place mats, belong in this optional area. A warming oven (see "A Shopper's Guide," page 96) might be handy here. The dishwasher should be nearby; some models even have integral trays that can be placed right into the flatware drawer.

SOME AUXILIARY CENTERS. Several additional kitchen areas have become so popular that they are quickly gaining work-center status. Before solidifying your plans, think about whether or not you wish to include one or more of these features:

- baking center
- breakfast/dining area
- menu-planning/office center
- built-in pantry or wine cellar
- entertainment center
- laundry/ironing center

Heights & clearances

As shown at top right, there are standard minimum clearances in a well-planned kitchen. These dimensions ensure enough space for a busy cook and some occasional cookie monsters; enough door clearance for free access to cabinets, dish-washer, and refrigerator; and enough traffic lanes for diners to comfortably enter and exit a breakfast nook. No entry doors, cabinet doors, or appliance doors should swing into each other.

Shown at bottom right are standard depths and heights for base and wall cabinets and shelves, plus recommended heights for stools, desktops, and eating counters.

Counter heights are based on kitchen industry standards but may be altered to fit the cook or cooks—provided that base cabinets and appliances can be accommodated. The formula for ideal food-preparation height is 2 to 3 inches below the cook's flexed elbows. For baking tasks, it's 5 inches below the elbows.

Turning corners

Corners are a problem when planning cabinet runs. Simply butting two cabinets together wastes storage space in the corner: on a base run, this adds up to a 24- by 24-inch waste; above, it's 12 by 12 inches.

Angled cabinets, blind cabinets, and lazy Susans (see pages 82–83) all supply corner solutions. Be sure that drawers and doors of adjacent units will open without banging into each other. Cabinet manufacturers offer so-called "filler strips" to cure this common woe; the strips separate cabinets by an inch or two.

STANDARD KITCHEN DIMENSIONS

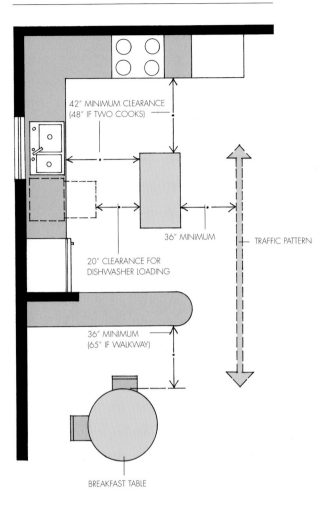

42" MINIMUM CLEARANCE (48" IF TWO COOKS)

20" CLEARANCE FOR DISHWASHER LOADING

36" MINIMUM

TRAFFIC PATTERN

36" MINIMUM (65" IF WALKWAY)

BREAKFAST TABLE

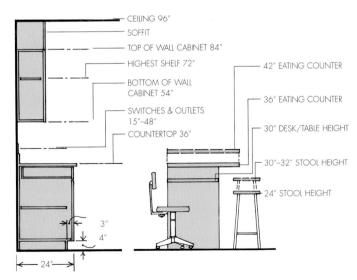

CEILING 96"
SOFFIT
TOP OF WALL CABINET 84"
HIGHEST SHELF 72"
BOTTOM OF WALL CABINET 54"
SWITCHES & OUTLETS 15"–48"
COUNTERTOP 36"

42" EATING COUNTER
36" EATING COUNTER
30" DESK/TABLE HEIGHT
30"–32" STOOL HEIGHT
24" STOOL HEIGHT

3"
4"
24"

design ideas

WITH A BASIC *floor plan now in mind, you can begin to fine-tune your decorating scheme. Wall and ceiling coverings, cabinetry, flooring, hardware, and even appliances are powerful tools for evoking both style and mood. Style effects are directly linked to color, pattern, texture, size, and shape.*

You'll find scores of design ideas beginning on page 28. Here, we introduce some reliable basic design concepts for you to use as starting points.

Do you want your new kitchen streamlined or unfitted? The high-tech design shown at right shows a minimalist's touch, sporting sealed concrete countertops, colorful European-like steel cabinets, floating shelves, and unrimmed sink. By contrast, the kitchen shown on the facing page features a furniture-like center island, a freestanding range, glass pendant fixtures, and earthy surfaces of maple, limestone, and tile.

What's your style?

A decorating style has physical characteristics that identify it with a particular region, era, or artistic movement—Colonial, English Victorian, Southwestern, Arts and Crafts, Art Deco, and so on. Because certain colors, materials, and decorative motifs are linked to certain historic decorating styles, they can be used to evoke the character of a period—or simply to personalize and give dignity to a bland modern room.

Representative kitchen styles include the following:

- Period (or traditional)
- Regional
- Country
- Romantic
- Contemporary (also high-tech)
- Eclectic

This said, rarely are styles slavish replicas of historical designs. More typically, designers select among elements that echo the mood of a

period or regional look. What matters is that you choose a style and mood you find sympathetic and comfortable. And if the kitchen is open to adjoining spaces, it should match or at least complement the overall look. Study the photos on pages 28–75—you may find style ideas there that you'd like to adapt to your own setting. Consumer and trade publications also offer helpful information on up-to-date decor.

Simple materials helped create this functional and attractive space. A rolled laminate backsplash yields a sleek look with no joint between the counter and the backsplash. Graceful curved cutouts make drawer pulls unnecessary. The concrete floor, broken up by 2 × 4s, is a balance of design and durability.

Looking at lines

Most kitchens incorporate different types of line—vertical, horizontal, diagonal, curved, and angular. But often one predominates and characterizes the design. Vertical lines give a sense of height, horizontal lines add width, diagonals suggest movement, and curved and angular lines impart grace and dynamism.

Continuity of lines gives a sense of unity to a design. Try an elevation (head-on) sketch of your proposed kitchen. How do the vertical lines created by the base cabinets, windows, doors, wall cabinets, and appliances fit together? It's not necessary for them to align perfectly, but you might consider small changes such as varying the width of a wall cabinet (without sacrificing storage) to line it up with the range, sink, or corresponding base cabinet.

You can follow a similar process to smooth out horizontal lines. Is the top of the window continuous with the top of the wall cabinets? If the window is just a few inches higher, you can either raise the cabinets or add trim and a soffit.

Weighing the scale

When the scale of kitchen elements is proportionate to the overall scale of the kitchen, the design seems harmonious. A small kitchen seems even smaller if fitted with large appliances and expanses of closed cabinets. Open shelves, large windows, and a simple overall design can visually enlarge such a room. Smaller objects arranged in a group help balance a large item, making it less obtrusive.

Studying shapes

Take a look at the shapes created by doorways, windows, cabinets, appliances, peninsula, island, and other elements in your kitchen. If these shapes are different, is there a basic sense of harmony? If you have an arch over a cooking niche, for example, you may want to repeat that shape in a doorway, on frame-and-panel cabinet doors, or in the trim of an open shelf. Or you can complement an angled peninsula by adding an angled corner cabinet or cooktop unit on the opposite wall.

Color concepts

The size and orientation of your kitchen, your personal preferences, and the mood you want to create all affect the selection of your color scheme. Light colors reflect light, making walls appear to recede; thus, decorating a small kitchen in light colors can make it seem more spacious. Dark colors absorb light and can make the ceiling feel lower or visually shorten a narrow room.

When considering colors for a small kitchen, remember that too much contrast has the same effect as a dark color: it reduces the sense of expansiveness. Contrasting colors work well for adding accents or drawing attention to interesting structural elements. But if you need to conceal a problem feature, it's best to use one color throughout the area.

Depending on the orientation of your kitchen, you may want to use warm or cool colors to balance the quality of natural light.

The earthy textures and soft colors of tumbled marble tiles are interspersed with brighter, random-pattern accent tiles in this backsplash. An eggplant-colored concrete countertop makes a bold, contemporary statement.

While oranges, yellows, and colors with a red tone impart a feeling of warmth, they also contract space. Blues, greens, and colors with a blue tone make an area seem cooler—and larger.

A light, monochromatic color scheme (using different shades of one color) is restful and serene. Contrasting colors add vibrancy and excitement to a design, though a color scheme with contrasting colors can be overpowering unless the tones of those colors are subdued. Another possibility is to include bright, intense color accents in furnishings and accessories that can be changed without too much trouble or cost.

After you narrow down your selections, make a sample board to see how your choices work together. Color charts for various appliances and fixtures are readily available, as are paint chips, fabric swatches, and wallpaper and flooring samples.

Remember that the color temperature and intensity and the placement of light fixtures will have an effect on overall color rendition. For details, see pages 108–109.

Texture & pattern

Textures and patterns work like color in defining a room's space and style. The kitchen's surface materials may include many different textures— from a shiny tile backsplash to rough oak cabinets to an appealingly irregular quarry-tile floor.

Rough textures absorb light, make colors look duller, and lend a feeling of informality. Smooth textures reflect light and tend to suggest elegance or modernity. Using similar textures helps unify a design and create a sustained mood.

Pattern choices must harmonize with the predominant style of the room. Although we usually associate pattern with wall coverings or cabinet doors, even natural substances like wood and stone create patterns.

While variety in texture and pattern adds interest, too much variety can be overstimulating. It's best to let a strong feature or dominating pattern be the focus of your design and choose other surfaces to complement rather than compete with it.

remodeling
realities

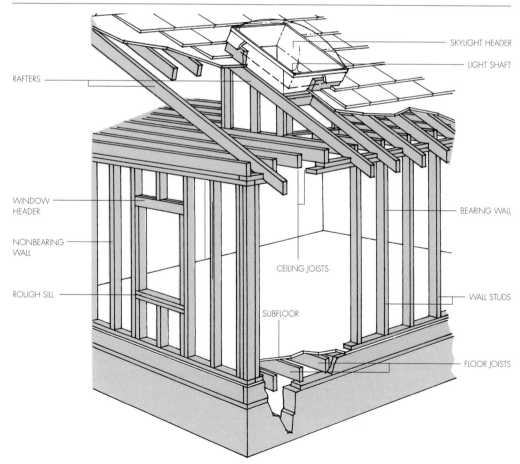

IF YOUR KITCHEN *requires only a new cooktop, a faucet, and some wallpaper to update it, you probably won't need to find out just what lurks behind those walls. But if you're relocating or adding appliances, installing a vent hood, or removing a wall, you'll have to bone up on some basic remodeling realities, whether or not you're hiring professional help. These next pages offer an overview of kitchen systems.*

STRUCTURAL FRAMING

SKYLIGHT HEADER

LIGHT SHAFT

RAFTERS

WINDOW HEADER

NONBEARING WALL

ROUGH SILL

BEARING WALL

CEILING JOISTS

WALL STUDS

SUBFLOOR

FLOOR JOISTS

Structural changes

If you're planning to open up space, add a skylight, or lay a heavy stone floor, your kitchen remodel may require some structural modifications.

As shown at left, walls are either bearing (supporting the weight of ceiling joists and/or second-story walls) or nonbearing. If you're removing all or part of a bearing wall, you must bridge the gap with a sturdy beam and posts. Nonbearing (also called partition) walls can usually be removed without too much trouble—unless pipes or wires are routed through them.

Doors and windows require special framing, as shown; the size of the header depends on the width of the opening and your local building codes. Skylights require similar cuts through ceiling joists and/or rafters.

Planning a vaulted or cathedral ceiling instead of ceiling covering and joists? You'll probably need to install a few beams to maintain structural soundness.

Hardwood, ceramic tile, and stone floors require very stiff underlayment. A solution is to beef up the floor joists and/or add additional plywood or particleboard subflooring on top. You may also need stronger floor framing to handle a large commercial range.

Plumbing restrictions

What if you wish to move the sink to the other side of the room or add a kitchen island with a vegetable sink or wet bar?

Generally, it's an easy job—at least conceptually—to extend existing water-supply pipes to a new sink or appliance. But if you're working on a concrete slab foundation, you'll need to drill through the slab or bring the pipes through the wall from another point above floor level.

Every house has a main soil stack. Below the level of the fixtures, it's your home's primary drainpipe. At its upper end, which protrudes through the roof, the stack becomes a vent. A new fixture located within a few feet of the existing main stack usually can be drained and vented directly by the stack. In some areas, a

PLUMBING PIPES

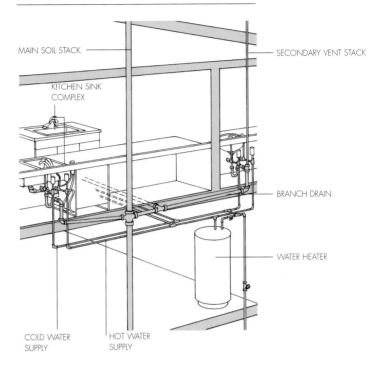

MAIN SOIL STACK

KITCHEN SINK COMPLEX

SECONDARY VENT STACK

BRANCH DRAIN

WATER HEATER

COLD WATER SUPPLY

HOT WATER SUPPLY

new island sink can be wet-vented (using an oversize branch drain as both drain and vent), though this is illegal in other areas. Sometimes a fixture located far from the main stack will require its own branch drain and a secondary vent stack of its own rising to the roof—an expensive proposition. Be sure to check your local codes for exact requirements.

When you convert from electricity to gas or simply relocate a gas appliance, keep in mind some basic guidelines. The plumbing code, or separate gas code, will specify pipe size (figured according to cubic-foot capacity and the length of pipe between the meter or storage tank and the appliance). All gas appliances should have name plates stamped with a numerical rating in BTUs per hour.

Each appliance must have a nearby code-approved shutoff valve with a straight handle so gas can be easily turned off during an emergency.

Electrical requirements

Electrical capacity is probably the problem most often overlooked by would-be remodelers. All those shiny new appliances take power to operate! In fact, the typical kitchen makeover requires three to five new circuits.

Requirements for electrical circuits serving a modern kitchen and dining area are clearly prescribed by the National Electrical Code (NEC). Plug-in outlets and switches for small appliances and the refrigerator must be served by a minimum of two 20-amp circuits. Light fixtures share one or more 15- or 20-amp circuits, which also run, as a rule, to the dining room, living room, or other adjacent space.

If you're installing a dishwasher and/or disposal, you'll need a separate 20-amp circuit for each. Most electric ranges use an individual 50-amp, 120/240-volt major appliance circuit. Wall ovens and a separate cooktop may share a 50-amp circuit. Kitchen receptacles must be protected by ground fault circuit interrupters (GFCIs) that cut off power immediately if current begins to leak anywhere along the circuit.

Older homes with two-wire service (120 volts only) of less than 100 amps simply can't support many major improvements. To add a new oven or dishwasher, you may well need to increase your service type and rating, which means updating the service entrance equipment.

ELECTRICAL WIRING

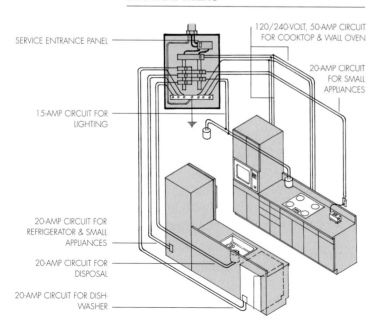

SERVICE ENTRANCE PANEL

120/240-VOLT, 50-AMP CIRCUIT FOR COOKTOP & WALL OVEN

20-AMP CIRCUIT FOR SMALL APPLIANCES

15-AMP CIRCUIT FOR LIGHTING

20-AMP CIRCUIT FOR REFRIGERATOR & SMALL APPLIANCES

20-AMP CIRCUIT FOR DISPOSAL

20-AMP CIRCUIT FOR DISH-WASHER

MECHANICAL SYSTEMS

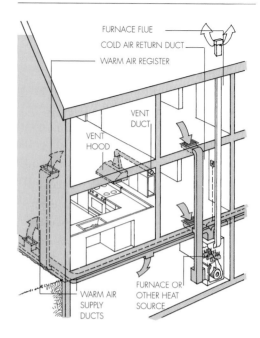

FURNACE FLUE
COLD AIR RETURN DUCT
WARM AIR REGISTER

VENT DUCT

VENT HOOD

WARM AIR SUPPLY DUCTS

FURNACE OR OTHER HEAT SOURCE

Mechanical (HVAC) systems

Heating, ventilation, and air-conditioning hardware—lumped together as "HVAC" systems—may all be affected by your proposed kitchen remodel. Changes will be governed either by your local plumbing regulations or by a separate mechanical code.

Air-conditioning and heating ducts are relatively easy to reroute, as long as you can gain access from a basement, crawl space, garage wall, or unfinished attic. Radiant-heat pipes or other slab-embedded systems may pose problems; check them out. Registers are usually easy to reposition; the toe space of base cabinets is a favorite spot for retrofits. Don't place any cold air returns in the new kitchen.

Are you planning a new freestanding range, a cooktop, wall ovens, or a built-in barbecue? You'll need to think about ventilation, providing either a hood above or a downdraft system exiting through the floor or an exterior wall. The downdraft system is especially apt for a new kitchen island or peninsula, but vent hoods are more efficient. See pages 98–99 for ventilation principles and options.

DOLLARS AND CENTS

How much will your new kitchen cost? According to the National Kitchen & Bath Association, the average figure is $22,100. This is, of course, only the sketchiest of estimates. You may simply need to replace countertops, add recessed downlights, reface your cabinets, or exchange a worn-out range to achieve a fresh look. On the other hand, extensive structural changes coupled with ultra-high-end materials and appliances could easily add up to $100,000.

As shown below, kitchen cabinets typically eat up 48 percent of the pie; labor comes in at around 16 percent; countertops add 13 percent; and, on the average, appliances, fixtures, and fittings tally another 12 percent. Structural, plumbing, and electrical changes all affect costs significantly.

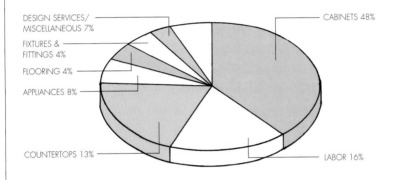

DESIGN SERVICES/ MISCELLANEOUS 7%
FIXTURES & FITTINGS 4%
FLOORING 4%
APPLIANCES 8%
COUNTERTOPS 13%
CABINETS 48%
LABOR 16%

How do you keep the budget under control? For starters, identify whether you're looking at a simple face-lift, a more extensive replacement, or a major structural remodel. Cabinet and appliance prices vary dramatically, depending on whether they're low-, middle-, high-, or ultra-high-end. Obtain ballpark figures in different categories, mull them over, then present your supplier, architect, or designer with a range of options and a bottom line with which you can be comfortable. You can, of course, save substantially by providing labor yourself—but be sure you're up to the task!

If you use the services of a design professional, expect to be charged either a flat fee or a percentage of the total cost of goods purchased (usually 10 to 15 percent). General contractors include their fees in their bids.

Don't make price your only criterion for selection. Quality of work, reliability, rapport, and on-time performance are also important. Ask professionals for the names and telephone numbers of recent clients. Call several and ask them how happy they were with the process and the results. Some may allow you to come and take a look at finished work.

gearing up

Oɴᴄᴇ ʏᴏᴜ'ᴠᴇ *worked out an efficient layout, planned your storage requirements, and decided on color and design schemes, it's time to draw up a revised floor plan. For help selecting new appliances, cabinets and countertops, flooring, and so on, see "A Shopper's Guide," beginning on page 77. Be sure to think about light fixtures and electrical switches or receptacles. And don't forget such finishing touches as doorknobs and drawer pulls, hinges and moldings, curtains and blinds—details that can really pull a design together.*

The final plan

Draw your new floor plan, or working drawing, the same way you did the existing plan (see page 8). On the new plan, include existing features you want to preserve and all the changes you're planning to make. If you prefer, you can hire a designer, drafter, or contractor to draw the final plan for you. Elevation sketches aren't usually required, but they'll prove helpful in planning the work.

For more complicated projects, your city or county building department may require additional or more detailed drawings of structural, plumbing, and wiring changes. You may also need to show areas adjacent to the kitchen so officials can determine how the project will affect the rest of your house. To discover just which building codes may govern your remodeling proj-

The owners of this urban kitchen wanted more space and a breakfast counter, too, but they had a problem: plumbing pipes ran from floor to ceiling directly through the area. Solution? The pipe run was boxed in and wrapped in classic white woodwork to match the frame-and-panel cabinets.

ect and learn whether a permit is required, check with your local building department.

If you do the ordering of materials, you'll need to compile a detailed master list. This will help you keep track of purchases and deliveries. For each item, specify the following information: name and model or serial number, manufacturer, source of material, date of order, expected delivery date, color, size or dimensions, quantity, price (including tax and delivery charge), and—where possible—a second choice.

Need help?

The listing below covers professionals in kitchen design and construction and delineates distinctions (although there's overlap) between architects, designers, contractors, and other professionals.

Finding the right help need not be daunting. In choosing a professional, look for someone who is technically and artistically skilled, has a proven track record, and is adequately insured against any mishaps on the job. It's also important to work with someone with whom you and your family feel comfortable. A kitchen remodel is more than just a construction project; it's a personal matter.

ARCHITECTS. Architects are state-licensed professionals with degrees in architecture. They're trained to create designs that are structurally sound, functional, and aesthetically pleasing. They also know construction materials, can negotiate bids from contractors, and can supervise the actual work. Many architects are members of the American Institute of Architects (AIA). If structural calculations must be made, architects can make them; other professionals need state-licensed engineers to design structures and sign working drawings.

If your remodel involves major structural changes, an architect should definitely be consulted. But some architects may not be as familiar with the latest in kitchen design and materials as other specialists.

KITCHEN DESIGNERS. These people know the latest trends in cabinets and appliances, but may lack the structural knowledge of the architect and the aesthetic skill of a good interior designer (see at right).

If you decide to work with a kitchen designer, look for a member of the National Kitchen & Bath Association (NKBA) or a Certified Kitchen Designer (CKD), a specialist certified by the NKBA. These associations have codes of ethics and sponsor continuing programs to inform members about the latest materials and techniques.

RETAIL SPECIALISTS. This category includes showroom personnel, building-center staff, and other retailers. Some are quite qualified and genuinely helpful. But others may be motivated simply to sell you more goods. If your kitchen needs only a minor face-lift, this help may be all you need. If you're tackling a large job, check qualifications carefully.

INTERIOR DESIGNERS. Even if you're working with an architect or kitchen designer, you may wish to call on the services of an interior designer for finishing touches. These experts specialize in the decorating and furnishing of rooms and can offer fresh, innovative ideas and advice. And through their contacts, a homeowner has access to materials and products not available at the retail level.

Some interior designers offer complete remodeling services, including the increasingly sophisticated field of lighting design. Many belong to the American Society of Interior Designers (ASID), a professional organization.

GENERAL CONTRACTORS. Contractors specialize in construction, although some have design skills and experience as well. General contractors may do all the work themselves, or they may assume responsibility for hiring qualified subcontractors, ordering construction materials, and seeing that the job is completed according to contract. Contractors can also secure building permits and arrange for inspections as work progresses.

When choosing a contractor, ask architects, designers, and friends for recommendations. To compare bids, contact at least three state-licensed contractors.

SUBCONTRACTORS. If you act as your own contractor, you will have to hire and supervise subcontractors for specialized jobs such as wiring, plumbing, and tiling. You'll be responsible for permits, insurance, and possibly even payroll taxes, as well as direct supervision of all the aspects of construction. Do you have the time and the knowledge required for the job? Be sure to assess your energy level realistically.

GREAT KITCHEN IDEAS

IN THE OLD DAYS, a picture was worth a thousand words. And regardless of the current exchange rate, photos are still the best way to show what's new in kitchen design. **I**N TERMS OF STYLE, these rooms represent as broad a palette as possible. You'll find European cabinets and components, French country motifs, classic brass, high-tech concrete, and stainless steel. But don't worry too much about sticking to one theme: creative kitchens often combine elements of several. **E**ACH REAL-LIFE situation is different, too. Most of these designs address special problems or requests, and some of these solutions may work for you. Many of the ideas can be combined or scaled up or down, depending on your needs. If it's individual units that catch your fancy, you'll find more details in "A Shopper's Guide," beginning on page 77.

high style

We OPEN our showcase with an overview of kitchen looks and layouts. There are big kitchens and small kitchens here, simple hardworking spaces and expansive rooms with the latest in amenities.

When planning, it's best to explore your space preferences early. Do you want your kitchen open or closed? The popular great room is simply any large space that houses the kitchen, eating area, and living areas, thus viewing the kitchen as an entertainment space and bringing family and friends together during meal preparation.

There are potential drawbacks. The open kitchen can seem "cold," and work areas must be blocked out carefully. Noise can be a problem, and privacy is obviously reduced. In remodeling, a great-room layout almost always means knocking out an existing wall or two. Some serious cooks are appalled by the idea of a space where they can't concentrate in solitude, or where messy pots are on view!

The two main poles of kitchen style are country and contemporary. Beyond that, there are period, geographical, romantic, gourmet, and eclectic styles. Hybrids abound. Many new designs strive to blend traditional looks with modern convenience. As a starting point, do you want things streamlined or unfitted? High-tech or homey? Do you wish to display kitchen goods and collectibles or hide them away? You'll see examples of all these approaches on the following pages.

The view through the column-flanked opening reveals an Arts-and-Crafts kitchen with dark oak flooring, stained cherry woodwork, and an unstained, furniture-like center island.

Cheery morning light pours into this French-bistro-inspired kitchen through both windows and a panel of glass blocks set between two steel pot racks. The compact plan includes a stainless steel-topped island for a food-prep sink and a granite-topped breakfast penin-sula (the main sink area lies just beyond). Hanging glass pendants and canary-colored plaster walls complete the picture.

Blending crisp modern
details with a thoroughly
traditional style, this open
kitchen revolves around its
curved, granite-topped
island. Additional textural
interest is provided by the
dark cherry counters, the
gleaming hardwood floor,
stainless-steel appliances, and
a subdued tile backsplash. A
white-painted bookcase (right)
adds a relaxed feel and makes
good use of a potentially
awkward corner wall.

This layout really goes with the flow. The kitchen was designed to be an integral part of an open living space that's frequently used for entertaining. Perimeter work areas, housed in furniture-grade cabinets topped with Italian marble, curve gracefully toward a high-ceilinged, skylit living room. The view in the opposite direction (left) shows a serving peninsula with wet bar, ice-maker, and lighted cabinets for glassware.

A house addition formed the shell for this beautifully detailed "colonial" kitchen. The antique range (shown below) was the starting point; its brick-lined surround and the homeowner's period collectibles occupy one wall, along with a built-in refrigerator concealed behind period-style doors. A long, fir-topped center island, equipped with food-prep sink, divides the range area from a window-lined dining alcove (left). Modern amenities (facing page) include a brick-lined pizza oven and a walk-in pantry with copious storage.

Country to the max, this small, U-shaped kitchen features waxed-pine cabinets that were designed as furniture, like the display hutch in the foreground. Diagonally laid 8-inch saltillo floor pavers lead to the main work area. Solid-surface countertops, leaded windows, ceiling timbers, and racks for pans and dried flowers keep the country look. Wall cabinets have novel fabric panels (shown at right) and include a "false front" of apothecary drawers (there are larger, more usable drawers behind).

A vintage 1920s range set the tone for this nostalgic white-on-white design. Hexagonal mosaic floor tiles, like those of a bygone ice-cream parlor, team with subway-style white wall tiles set in a classic running-bond pattern. Off camera are modern wall ovens and other non-'20s conveniences.

The prominent location—adjacent to the foyer and stairway—of this kitchen and dining area inspired its sophisticated look that bridges the gap between formal and family friendly. Because the kitchen cabinets are such an integral part of the design, they are trimmed to look like large pieces of furniture. Segmented columns, bullnose cornice molding, and recessed panel doors further enhance their old-world character.

An open, ultramodern, white-on-white kitchen is part of a "zero tolerance" house design—no moldings, no fudging, no extraneous details to interrupt the clarity of the look. The kitchen nestles behind the dining area, concealed by a high white knee wall. Euro-style laminate cabinets fit above custom 24-inch German wall tiles, which also form the countertops. The dark gray sealed-concrete floor has radiant heat underneath. Low-voltage cable lights do a spare but playful dance overhead.

Expressively casual, this remodeled bungalow kitchen is tiny, unfitted, and exuberant at the same time. Natural cherry cabinets are mixed with forest green units, pockets of open shelving, curtain fronts, concrete counters, a solid-surface apron sink, handmade tile, and a quilted-steel backing in the cooking area. The floor is another stylish throwback—real linoleum! The modern range has a downdraft vent, which saves the space of an overhead hood. Another space-saving trick: the refrigerator, out of view to the left, is recessed into the wall of an adjacent utility room.

This was a small, dark kitchen, redone on a budget. Twin greenhouse windows flanking the reconditioned range bring in daylight and make the space seem larger. New surfaces include fruitwood-stained maple cabinets with Italian pulls and counters made from inexpensive machined floor tiles with tight, easy-to-clean grout lines. A granite-topped island on casters adds counter surface but can be pushed aside to open up the space.

Attention to detail and a mix
of materials make this new house
on Kiawah Island, South
Carolina feel as though it's been
there for years. In the kitchen
and breakfast room, a 9-foot-
tall pine cabinet offers a pleasing
counterpoint to a large island
crafted of cherry and granite.
The pressed-tin ceiling was
painted dark green to animate
an octagonal dining area. A
subtle change in the floor pattern
echoes the room's geometry.

Formal as can be, this kitchen
is defined by its long, limestone-
topped island and ceiling-hung
wall cabinets. The cabinets'
two-sided glass doors have
frames that follow the arched
window by the sink; their glass
shelves are accented by small
built-in downlights. Cabinet
wood is lightly pickled and
stippled to support the look of
the heavily fossilized counter
surfaces. A band of gray-green
trim tile along the backsplash
adds a muted note of contrast.
French doors lead to an outdoor entertainment area.

*Here the idea was to create
an open, gracious, great-room
kitchen where guests would feel
as comfortable as family. The
range surround, cast in concrete,
is matched in tone by limestone-
colored concrete countertops and
plastered walls. Cherry cabinetry
and terra-cotta pavers lend
warmth to the decor; so does the
fireplace at far right.*

Warmed and brightened by sky-
lights and a bank of windows,
this remodeled kitchen provides
modern-day amenities in a
19th-century Charlottesville,
Virginia farmhouse. Two sinks
afford separate areas for cook-
ing and cleanup. Floors are
heart pine. A grid of square
columns and beams provides a
sense of separation between the
kitchen and breakfast room.

on the surface

SURFACES are a major element of kitchen style. In fact, many popular styles are defined, at least in part, by the countertops, floor coverings, and wall and ceiling treatments you choose. Also factor in the finishes on fixtures and appliances.

Surfaces can be hard or soft, bright or subdued, glossy or matte. Light surfaces spread light, dark ones absorb it. Many new kitchen designs lean toward quieter colors but gain impact with more sensational textures.

Just a few years ago, the average countertop, usually laminate, included a 4-inch lip on the back. Today's higher backsplashes, however, often feature materials that are found there alone. Geometric or hand-painted art tiles are popular choices. Stone tiles are an economical alternative to solid granite or marble. Stainless-steel and mirrored surfaces are showing up in high-tech surroundings.

Faux-finished walls and ceiling, fir floor, plus wall and floor stenciling keep a 1937-vintage range comfortable in its modern surroundings, which include a granite eating counter and stylish, stainless-steel pendant lights.

Clean, simple diamond accents are formed from blue glass mosaics embedded in a plastered backsplash above the kitchen range.

Beyond aesthetic considerations, you should weigh the physical characteristics of surfaces. Most kitchens take a lot of wear and tear. Is your countertop choice water resistant, durable, and easy to maintain? Is the floor hard to walk on, noisy, or slippery underfoot?

Your kitchen will probably include a good bit of wall space. What's the best kind of paint for kitchen walls? Latex is easy to work with, but alkyd paint (often called oil-base paint) provides high gloss and will hang on a little harder. Look for products labeled gloss or semigloss if you want a tough, washable wall finish.

Maximum impact at minimum cost was the challenge. The choice, according to the project designer, was "to go with color, period—to make that work as the detailing." Fir trim and stainless-steel appliances team with vibrant paints, stains, green-laminate countertops, and charcoal vinyl floor tiles.

At first glance, you might not guess that this modern kitchen sits in the heart of the historic district of Chapel Hill, North Carolina. The house was built in 1911, but its remodeled kitchen reflects the modern sensibility of the owner's native Denmark. Two islands, topped with black granite, ensure plenty of space for a family of six to gather.

Outdoor sign-making techniques helped create these cabinet doors. Test negatives were made by putting tree branches and leaves on white paper and spray-painting them black; then the manufacturer was asked to render the favorite composition onto metal in two different shades of green. The inserts fit into the cabinets' cedar door frames just like standard panels. Counters and backsplash are slate-patterned plastic laminate.

This new kitchen, designed to look older, blends concrete countertops and matching textured plaster with colorful slate backsplash tiles, flat-paneled cabinets, and floating, open shelves. Rustic flooring is of hand-hewn pearwood planks. Wall cabinet panels are gleaming wire mesh, matching the metallic accents of the modular cooktop, vent hood, drawer pulls, and pot-filling faucet.

Reedlike patterns swirl across these cabinet-door panels of stainless steel. The coarse but almost organic appearance was achieved by repeated passes with a hand-held grinder. Because light plays off the multifaceted surface, the doors seem to change as you pass by.

Cows amble across a
pastoral vista and stare
placidly out at the own-
ers of this hand-painted
backsplash mural. Large
tiles with thin grout lines
keep the composition
unified. The countertop
is granite; cabinets
are maple.

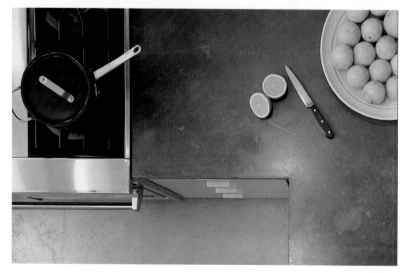

Sealed concrete
makes a handsome,
durable surface for
countertops and floor.

*Vibrant colors from an earthy palette
set the tone for this kitchen, where the
floor and the backsplash include
rows of tumbled marble interspersed
with glazed accent tiles. This remodel
balances traditional features—
white-paneled cabinetry and beaded
wainscoting—with contemporary
elements such as concrete counters
and stainless-steel appliances.*

great kitchen ideas

storage solutions

CONSIDER the kitchen cabinet. Most often it's either stained brown or painted white. But today's homeowners want more zip, so cabinet manufacturers are developing more venturesome designs to go with a rapidly expanding spectrum of surfacing choices and appliances. Architects and designers are using vivid colors, sculptural shapes, and inventive finishing techniques to turn cabinets into memorable kitchen furniture.

Do you want seamless European-style cabinets or traditional faceframe units? (For further details, see pages 78–85.) Consider the pros and cons of open shelves: on the plus side, they offer readily accessible and pleasantly casual storage and display space. In the minus column, remember that open goods get dusty—and that anything untidy is always in view. Glass-fronted wall cabinets are similarly open to view, especially if you choose clear rather than semiopaque glazing.

Floating shelves, a coat of rich indigo paint, and a collection of vintage pottery transform a once-bland kitchen wall into a stunning showcase.

The deep green of the glass-fronted cabinets, the four-square paint detail on each drawer front, and the golden glow of the maple counters and back-splash turn the corner of this kitchen into a dramatic display area for crockery.

Pullout drawers and shelves provide handy storage for kitchen goods. Appliance garages, fronted with flip-up or tambour doors, can help corral food processors and other small accessories. Kitchen islands are also great places to add storage. No room? Consider a movable cart with a butcher-block top.

What about a food pantry? Place one inside a cabinet run or look to a more remote location. Are there two cooks and multiple prepping and cooking centers? One solution, though potentially space-consuming, is to store multiple versions of basic utensils and spices.

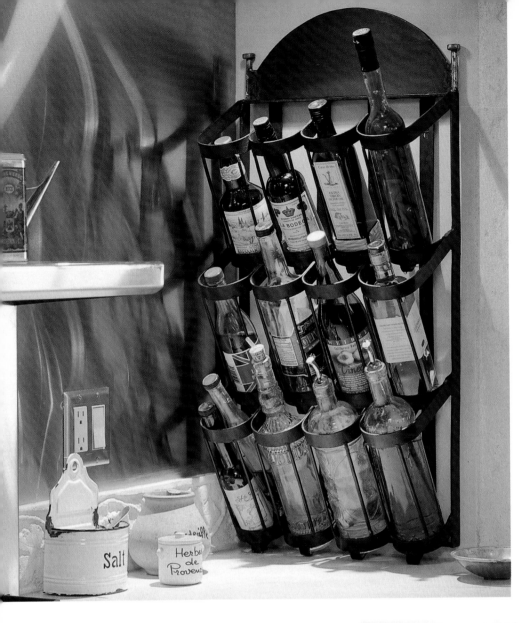

A wrought-iron wine rack, discovered while window-shopping down a wine-country street, takes on new life rangeside as a holster for flavored oils and other chef's accoutrements.

A pine pantry armoire with Shaker-simple lines contrasts with formal cherry cabinetry elsewhere in the kitchen. Behind the upper doors is a battery of pullouts on heavy-duty drawer guides; below are partitioned drawers, including a stainless-steel bread insert. The custom unit has a crown molding at top and sits on furniture-style "legs."

Tight inside corners are always trouble: either you give up the space on one side, or the opposing drawers smack into each other. This two-sided, arrow-shaped custom unit offers a fresh solution.

It would be hard to find a more stylish set of storage bins than these hand-crafted, slatted creations, housed in an island that faces the main kitchen sink.

It looks like a blank cabinet end—but it's really the cabinet "door" that's the dummy. Inside is a compact, orderly pantry with ample, adjustable shelves and wire-fronted door racks.

Today's emphasis on recycling brings its challenges. How do you integrate potentially messy holding bins into an otherwise seamless kitchen design? This elegant solution is located at the end of a long kitchen island, facing away from the side most visible. The lipped plastic trash containers sit inside drawer cutouts and slide in and out as needed on sturdy drawer guides.

A *brick furnace flue,
uncovered during the
remodeling of a
small country kitchen,
becomes an earthy
backdrop for a
redwood trellis—
originally designed
for clematis or roses
but now sprouting
copper pots.*

*Held secure by stacked
plate rails crafted of
wrought iron and
heart pine, an array
of French and Italian
pottery collected by the
owner on her travels
assumes pride of place
in this kitchen. Once
wasted space below
now accommodates
deep drawers that
hold large items.
Baskets offer easy
access to the cubbyholes
low on the wall.*

*In this hardworking
remodeled kitchen,
there's plenty of storage
space for pans near
the microwave (near
right) and under the
cooktop (far right).*

bright ideas

No MATTER HOW efficient its layout, a kitchen with poor lighting is an unpleasant and tiring place to work. A good lighting plan creates shadowless, glare-free illumination for the entire room as well as bright light for specific tasks.

Daylight can enter a kitchen through windows, skylights, doors, or all three. For more even light, consider using two windows on adjacent walls or adding a skylight. Prefabricated greenhouse units, often placed be-hind sinks and countertops, are attractive space-stretchers and come with shelves for pots and planters; some also have sides or tops that open for ventilation. Similarly, bay and bow windows expand space and add light beside breakfast nooks and dining alcoves. Glass blocks let in soft, diffused light while providing privacy, security, and insulation. When it comes to linking the kitchen with a sunny deck or garden, French or sliding doors are unrivaled.

A sleek white kitchen is viewed from the entrance hall through an interior "window," which provides discreet display space with curving glass shelves and a halogen downlight.

This remodel is organized around a dramatic new pointed dormer window, almost Gothic in feeling, that rises from behind the sink to the very peak of the gable. The new window frames a view of trees and dominates the white-painted kitchen, flooding it with daylight.

You'll want strong, shadowless artificial light right over each kitchen work area. If your counter-tops, range, cooktop, and work spaces are well-lighted, general illumination need only be bright enough to ensure safe movement about the room. Architectural coves (built-in uplights) above the cabinets are a good way to supply a soft wash of ambient light. With multiple sources and dimmer controls, you can turn up the light full-throttle when working or gently subdue it after hours. When choosing kitchen fixtures, keep in mind that they'll need frequent cleaning.

This kitchen combines sunlight and storage in a single glass cabinet system. Only the cooktop's hood and venting mechanism are opaque. The rest of the wall consists of glass shelves sandwiched between two translucent vertical layers: frosted, rimless glass door panels at the front, and a wall of translucent panels along the exterior of the house.

*Factory-made, wood-framed
windows were ganged
to brighten and visually
expand a once-dark kitchen
with potential garden views.
Fixed panes align above
and below tall casement
windows in the 8-foot-
square window wall. The
shapes repeat in an adjacent
3-foot-wide French door.*

A *custom-designed greenhouse addition lends an airy, outdoor feel and plenty of light to the adjacent kitchen. Low-voltage cable lights fill in at night—and, occasionally, during high-contrast daylight hours. Their thin wire supports and decorative shades float unobtrusively while adding a touch of fun.*

The owner of this kitchen (part of a remodeled old winery) wanted lots of light, but the raised ceiling made it a challenging task. Stylish red Italian pendants, each housing tiny but efficient halogen bulbs, solved the problem and defined the space. Electrical conduit, painted white, leads from the roofline down to the fixtures, which were originally designed to be ceiling-mounted.

Incandescent bulbs on continuous track strips run through the soffit area above wall cabinets and backlight "etched" arrangements of bundled twigs. The lights provide enough illumination for people to negotiate the kitchen at night when other light sources are off.

In this kitchen, available light is maximized by two rows of windows on the north-facing wall. A variety of electric light sources fill in: fluorescent tubes both under and over the cabinets, MR-16 downlights, and 100-watt A-bulbs in decorative Italian glass pendants. Incandescent strip lights add a warm glow to the display niche over the refrigerator.

elegant options

As LIFE speeds up, many of us are spending more home time in the kitchen. It's natural that the space is being redefined to include such extras as breakfast banquettes, dining tables, message centers or office desks, and comfortable sitting areas. Correspondingly, such standard living-room features as fireplaces, media centers, and art displays are moving here, too.

Kitchen islands are serving as space dividers, storage lockers, wet bars, eating counters, and repositories for school projects and business reports alike. Islands also figure importantly in multi-cook and specialized work stations. A baking center might benefit from a stone-topped surface that's lower than adjacent countertops. Kitchen entertaining calls for chairs or stools, a serving center, and perhaps a wet bar.

On the office front, is there space for a computer, if needed? Phone and fax? Standard desk height is 30 inches; keyboard surfaces are usually slightly lower. How will you hide the inevitable clutter?

Media centers are entering this room now. Maybe you'd like built-in audio speakers connected to a central home system (it's a good idea to have at least a separate volume control in the kitchen). Or you might plan a large-screen TV or full-blown home theater adjacent to a great room's comfortable sitting area.

Increasingly, kitchen additions are planned with direct access to the garden or patio through a set of glazed patio doors.

A triangular peninsula works for kitchen prep and quick meals in a space too small for a freestanding island. It also bars guests from wandering into the kitchen, but still allows cross-counter conversation with the cook.

A formal espresso bar and serving area makes perfect use of this detached kitchen corner. Dish cabinets are cherry; the countertop and integral sink are patinated copper. Below the espresso machine, which is permanently mounted, is a handy ice-maker for those wanting cold drinks rather than hot.

A mother and designer needed a work space that would allow her to keep track of both dinner and her energetic offspring. The answer was a bank of built-ins made from the same maple as the kitchen cabinets and living-room units beyond. A pullout (shown at right) houses a sewing machine and typewriter and extends beyond base cabinets, ready for action.

As today's kitchens become central in both daily and entertainment operations, more families want media centers incorporated into their design. Here, a large-screen TV (it can be concealed behind cabinet doors) fills the space above the refrigerator. The view from the island's seating is great.

The broad, granite-topped peninsula angling out from this kitchen's main wall is a sleek, hardworking room divider. One side functions as an informal breakfast area. The other is all business, because that's where an author creates the elegant pastries that star in her cookbooks. The polished-granite top is 4 feet wide and more than 11 feet long—providing ample room for bowls, mixers, rolled-out dough, and baking sheets. The counter's cool surface, a comfortable 35 inches off the floor, is great for working with dough. An electric oven is built into one end of the peninsula, but the kitchen also contains one gas and one convection oven.

Ingenious storage solutions also help with serious baking. Shown on this page, at top left, a 35-inch-tall, roll-around island neatly stacks as many as 17 baking sheets. A 24-inch-wide, 30-inch-long, 4¼-inch-deep drawer (top right) also pulls its own weight, with com-partments that house a large array of baking supplies. Shown at bottom left is the owner's rolling pin collection. A shallow, egg-wide (1¼ inches) trough (lower right) machined into the granite countertop stops any ovoid wanderers.

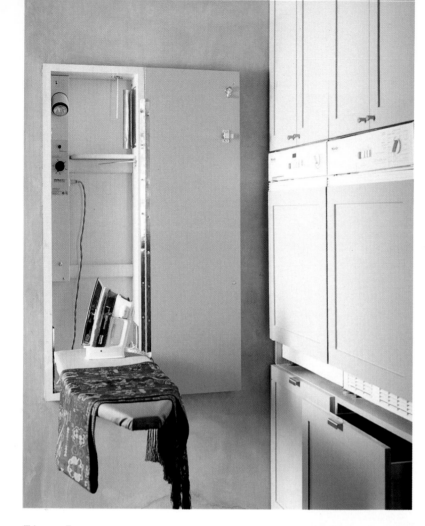

A handsomely trimmed upholstered banquette fits neatly into one end of this traditional kitchen. The dining area's back wall, divided by plate rails, displays a colorful tableware collection. Angling across the corner is a cabinet with built-in wine storage.

Trim new European washer and dryer units blend seamlessly into a floor-to-ceiling cabinet. This laundry area includes a pullout hamper and a recessed ironing board unit, complete with both a task light and an electrical outlet for the iron. The board disappears behind a door when not in use.

A benevolent cherub presides over an earthy brick fireplace that's snugged into this kitchen corner. The scrolled acanthus-leaf ornament echoes its lines.

A SHOPPER'S GUIDE

FRAMELESS laminate cabinets, solid-surface countertops, batch-feed garbage disposals, halogen cooktops, low-voltage wall washers—enough! The inexperienced shopper can be overwhelmed with the latest in gleaming stainless or bright enameled kitchen components. THAT'S WHERE this chapter can help. To keep things simple, we focus on one element at a time: cabinets, countertops, sinks, appliances, flooring, windows, and light fixtures. Color photos show the latest styles; text and comparison charts give you the working knowledge to brave the appliance center, to communicate with an architect or designer, or simply to replace that dingy old-fashioned countertop. ARMED WITH the basics, it's usually easy to go on to the fine points. And you can often borrow literature, samples, or swatches to study at home for color, size, and stylistic compatibility.

Cabinets

FROM FRAME TO FRAMELESS, THE OPTIONS ARE ENDLESS

Cabinets are the key element in kitchen storage. They set the tone of the room's decorative personality and form the backbone of its organization. For this reason—and because they represent the largest single investment in a new kitchen—it is important to study the many options available before making a decision.

Traditional or European-style?

The two basic cabinet construction styles are frame and frameless.

Traditional American cabinets mask the raw front edges of each box with a 1-by-2 "faceframe." Doors and drawers then fit in one of three ways: flush; partially offset, with a lip; or completely overlaying the frame.

The outer edges of the faceframe can be planed and shaped (called "scribing") according to individual requirements. Since the faceframe covers up the basic box, thinner or lower-quality wood can be used in its sides—somewhat decreasing the cost. But the frame takes up space and reduces the size of the openings, so drawers or slide-out accessories must be significantly smaller than the full width of the cabinet—somewhat decreasing storage capacity.

Europeans, when faced with postwar lumber shortages, came up with "frameless" cabinets. A simple trim strip covers raw edges, which butt directly against one another. Doors and drawers often fit to within

CABINET CLOSEUPS

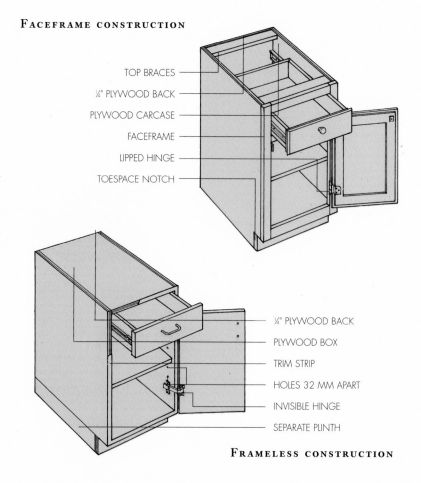

FACEFRAME CONSTRUCTION

TOP BRACES
¼" PLYWOOD BACK
PLYWOOD CARCASE
FACEFRAME
LIPPED HINGE
TOESPACE NOTCH

¼" PLYWOOD BACK
PLYWOOD BOX
TRIM STRIP
HOLES 32 MM APART
INVISIBLE HINGE
SEPARATE PLINTH

FRAMELESS CONSTRUCTION

⅛ inch of each other, revealing a thin sliver of the trim. Interior components, such as drawers, can be sized practically to the full dimensions of the box.

Another big difference: frameless cabinets typically have a separate toespace pedestal, or plinth. This allows you to set counter heights specifically to your liking, stack base units, or make use of space at floor level.

The terms "system 32" and "32-millimeter" refer to precise columns of holes drilled on the inside faces of many frameless cabinets. These holes are generally in the same places, no matter what cabinets you buy, and interchangeable components such as door hinges, drawer guides, shelf pins, and pullout baskets just plug right into them.

Cabinet doors and drawers set the look. The styles here include classic raised-panel fronts with bright white lacquer finish (upper left); frameless, overlay-style doors made from ash (upper right); and flat-panel, faceframe construction in vertical-grain fir (lower right).

Stock, custom, or semi-custom?

Cabinets are manufactured and sold in three different ways. The type you choose will affect the cost, overall appearance, and workability of your kitchen.

STOCK CABINETS. Buy your kitchen "off-the-shelf" and save—if you're careful. Mass-produced, standard-sized cabinets are the least expensive way to go, and they can be a good choice if you clearly understand the cabinetry you need for your kitchen. As the name implies, the range of sizes is limited.

Even so, you can always specify door styles, direction of door swing, and whether side panels are finished. And you can sometimes get options

COMPARING CABINETS

	Stock	Custom	Semi-custom
Where to buy	Lumberyards, home centers, appliance stores, some showrooms (most stock is made in this country).	Few cabinetmakers have showrooms; most offer pictures of completed jobs. Be safe: visit some installations.	These cabinets are mainly showroom items, but some are found in home centers and department stores.
Who designs	You should, because the clerk helping you may know less about cabinets than you do. Don't order if you're at all unsure.	You; your architect, builder, or kitchen designer; or the maker (but be careful: cabinetmakers aren't necessarily designers).	The better (and more expensive) the line, the more help you get. Top-of-the-line suppliers design your whole kitchen.
Cost range	Less than the two other choices, but you'll still swallow hard when you see the total. Look for heavy discounts at home centers, but pay attention to craftsmanship.	Very wide; depends, as with factory-made boxes, on materials, finishes, craftsmanship, and options you choose.	A basic box can cost about what stock does, but each upgrade in door and drawer style and finish boosts the cost considerably.
Options available	Only options may be door styles, hardware, and door swing—but check the catalog; some lines offer a surprising range.	You can often—but not always—get the same options and European-made hardware that go in semi-custom cabinets.	Most lines offer choices galore—including variations in basic sizes and cabinets for corners. Check showrooms and study catalogs.
Materials used	Cheaper lines may use doors of mismatched or lower-quality woods, composite, or thinner laminates that photo-simulate wood.	Anything you specify, but examine samples. Methods vary by cabinetmaker; look at door and drawer hardware in a finished kitchen.	Factory-applied laminates and catalyzed varnishes are usually of high quality and durable. Medium-density fiberboard is the quality alternative for wood in non-showing parts of the basic box.
Delivery time	You may be able to pick up cabinets at a warehouse the same day you order. Wait is generally shorter than for other types.	Figure five weeks or longer, depending on job complexity, number of drawers, and finishes. Allow extra time.	Five to eight weeks is typical, whether cabinets are American or imported, but delivery can actually take up to six months. Order early.
Installation & service	Depends on where you buy; supplier may recommend a contractor. Otherwise, you install yourself. Service is virtually nonexistent.	In most cases, the maker installs. Buy from an established shop and you should have no trouble getting service.	Better lines are sold at a price that includes installation and warranty. Some cabinets are virtually guaranteed for life.
Other considerations	You often pay in full up front, giving you little recourse if cabinets are shipped incorrectly. Be sure order is clear and complete.	Make sure the bid you accept is complete—not just a basic cost-per-foot or cost-per-box charge.	With some manufacturers, if cabinets are wrong, you'll wait as long for the right parts to arrive as you did in the first place.

and add-ons such as breadboards, sliding shelves, wine racks, and special corner units.

A recent development, the so-called RTA ("ready-to-assemble") cabinet costs even less than other stock units, but requires some basic tools and elbow grease to put together. An RTA cabinet is shown on the facing page.

You may see stock lines heavily discounted at some home centers. But buying such cabinets can be a lot like doing your own taxes: you may find you're lacking the knowledgeable help that could clarify the possibilities and save you money.

CUSTOM CABINETS. Many people still have a cabinetmaker come to their house and measure, then return to the cabinet shop and build custom cases, drawers, and doors.

Custom cabinet shops can match old cabinets, size truly oddball configurations, and accommodate complexities that can't be handled with stock or semi-custom cabinets. A skilled craftsperson can create kitchen woodwork that looks like fine furniture. Such jobs, however, may cost

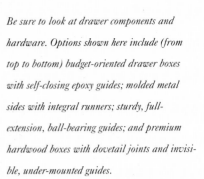

READY-TO-ASSEMBLE (RTA) CABINET

considerably more than medium-line stock or semi-custom cabinets.

SEMI-CUSTOM CABINETS. Between stock and custom cabinets are "semi-custom" or "custom modular" units, which can sometimes combine the best of both worlds. They are manufactured, but they are of a higher grade and offer more design flexibility than stock cabinets. Not surprisingly, they cost more, too.

Semi-custom systems come in a wide range of sizes, with many options within each size. You can change virtually everything on these basic modules: add sliding shelves; replace doors with drawers; set a matching hood unit over the cooktop; add wire baskets, flour bins, appliance garages, and pullout pantries. If necessary, heights, widths, and depths can be modified to fit almost any design.

Be advised, though: because these cabinets are configured to order and because most are imported from abroad, they could take longer to materialize than custom units from a local cabinetmaker. Order as much ahead as possible.

Judging quality

To determine the quality of a cabinet, first look closely at the drawers. They

take more of a beating than any other part. Several designs are shown. You'll pay a premium for such details as solid-wood drawer boxes, dovetail joints, or full-extension, ball-bearing guides.

Door hinges are also critical hardware elements. European or "invisible" hinges are most trouble-free. Choose these unless you want the period look of surface hardware. Check for adjustability; invisible hinges should be able to be reset and fine-tuned with the cabinets in place.

Most cabinet boxes are made from sheet products like plywood, particleboard (plain or laminated), or medium-density fiberboard. Solid lumber is sometimes used, but is usually reserved for doors and drawer faces.

Hardwood plywood is surfaced with attractive wood veneers on face and back. The higher the face grade, the more you'll pay. Particleboard costs less, weighs more, and is both weaker and more prone to warping and moisture damage than plywood. Generally, particleboard cabinets are faced with either high-pressure plastic laminates (see page 86) or a softer material called melamine. Medium-density fiberboard (MDF), a denser, furniture-grade particleboard, is tougher,

BASE CABINET OPTIONS

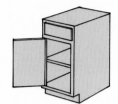

STANDARD BASE CABINET

DRAWER UNIT

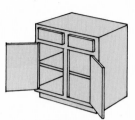

DOUBLE CABINET

DROP-IN RANGE BASE

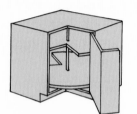

LAZY SUSAN BASE

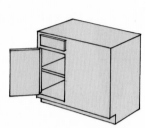

BLIND CORNER BASE

OVEN CABINET

REFRIGERATOR CABINET

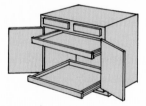

PULLOUT SHELVES

FALSE SINK FRONT

END SHELVES

ROUNDED END CABINET

PANTRY PACK

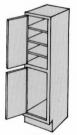

UTILITY CABINET

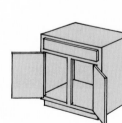

SINK OR RANGE BASE

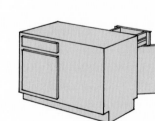

TWO-SIDED (ISLAND OR PENINSULA) CABINET

smoother, and available with high-quality hardwood veneers.

Make sure laminate and edge banding are thick enough not to peel at the corners and edges. "Once a cheap cabinet starts peeling," one shop warned, "that's it."

What choices are available?

The illustrations on these two pages show many basic cabinet units. You'll find variations on these in most lines.

The three main cabinet categories are base, wall, and tall or special-use. Because it's more economical to build with standardized dimensions, sizes tend to be consistent from line to line. Cabinet sizes must also match standard fixtures and appliances.

BASE CABINETS. Base cabinets combine storage space with working surface. Though usually equipped with only one top drawer, some base cabinets have three or four drawers, making them particularly useful near the sink, range, or refrigerator. "Sink" units have a false drawer front or a tilt-out drawer at the top.

Standard dimensions are 24 inches deep by 34½ inches high; the addition of a countertop raises them to 36 inches. In width, base cabinets range from about 9 to 48 inches, increasing in increments of 3 inches from 9 to 36 inches and in increments of 6 inches after that.

WALL CABINETS. Usually screwed to studs in the walls, these cabinets can also be hung from ceiling joists over peninsula and island installations. Wall cabinets come as single or double units and in various specialty configurations.

Typically 12 inches deep, wall cabinets can vary in width from about 9 to 48 inches. Though the most frequently used heights are 15, 18, and 30 inches, units actually range from 12 to 36 or more inches high. The shorter cabinets are typically mounted above refrigerators, ranges, and sinks. The tallest ones extend to high soffits or ceilings.

SPECIAL-USE UNITS. Manufacturers also produce a variety of special-purpose cabinets. You can buy cabinets with cutouts for sinks, built-in ranges, wall ovens, or microwaves. Island and pantry units also fall into this category.

Perhaps more options exist for corners than for any other kitchen cabinet space. These include angled units with larger doors, double-door units that provide full access to the L-shaped space, and lazy Susans or slide-out accessories that bring items forward from the back recesses of the space.

Getting help

The cabinets are only part of the puzzle. When you buy them, some of what you're paying for is varying degrees of help with the design.

A designer will help you figure out how you'll use the kitchen. Some retailers will give you a questionnaire (much like the one on page 9) to pin-

WALL CABINET OPTIONS

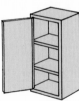

STANDARD WALL CABINET

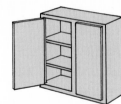

DOUBLE WALL CABINET

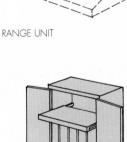

RANGE UNIT

FOLD-OUT PANTRY

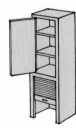

APPLIANCE GARAGE

APPLIANCE GARAGE

SLATTED DIVIDERS

BLIND CORNER CABINET

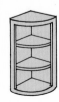

OPEN SHELVES

CURVED END CABINET

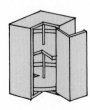

ANGLED LAZY SUSAN UNIT

ANGLED CABINET

WHAT ABOUT REFACING?

If your goal is just to update your present kitchen, and/or if you're on a tight budget, you might consider a speedier, cost-effective alternative to replacing your cabinets: refacing them.

Basically, "refacing" means just that. A specialty company or cabinetmaker removes existing doors and drawer fronts and replaces them with new ones. Visible surfaces like cabinet ends, edge banding, and faceframes are finished to match; the results look as if you'd replaced the entire cabinet system.

When is refacing a good idea? If the basic boxes are in good shape and you're satisfied with your current layout, this could be an attractive possibility. You can usually choose from a broad range of door and drawer styles, hardware, and finishes. Typically, the company's representative will show you samples, take measurements, and return for the installation. Refacers probably won't work on cabinet interiors, so you may wish to clean or paint these first.

Where can you locate refacing firms? Look in the yellow pages under Cabinet Refinishing & Refacing or Kitchen Cabinets & Equipment. Or check large home centers or lumberyards; some offer these services or can steer you in the right direction.

point what's unsatisfactory about your current kitchen, how often you do any specialty cooking, whether your guests always end up in the kitchen, whether you buy food in bulk, and other clues to a final design that really suits the way you live.

Pick a "look," then shop for it; compare features, craftsmanship, budget, and cost. Some designers represent a particular line, so shop around to get an idea of what's currently available.

Your existing floor plan (see page 8) is the best aid you can offer a designer. Some staff designers in showrooms will do a new cabinet plan for you, applying the charge against the purchase price of the cabinets. Some showrooms use computer renderings to help customers visualize the finished kitchen—with prices for different cabinet options just a keystroke away.

And what will all this cost?

There are no figures after "Cost range" in the chart on page 80. Why? The wide and changing range of styles—and prices—makes buying cabinets much like buying a car. Like car makers, every manufacturer or cabinetmaker picks a slot of the market, then offers various styles and options that build upward from a base price.

Dark-stained cabinets visually shrank the kitchen (above left). After the original doors were removed, the installer covered the existing shells with white plastic laminate, then routed out the openings. The final, room-brightening transformation was adding the new white doors and drawers (below left).

A CORNUCOPIA OF CABINET PULLS

Know your budget. You'll quickly find out what kinds of cabinets you can afford; with your plan in hand, you can get a basic price for standard cabinets relatively easily. But extras will drastically alter the quote—so the same basic cabinet can end up costing a number of different prices. Bids should be full quotes based on a fully specified room sketch listing the options desired in each cabinet. Is installation to be included? If so, spell it out.

Within each line, costs are largely determined by the nature of the doors and drawers you choose. The simplest, least expensive option is often a flat or "slab" door, popular in seamless European designs. Frame-and-panel designs are more traditional and come in many versions, including raised panel (both real and false), arched panel, beaded panel, and recessed or flat panel.

Are cabinet pulls included? If not, you'll pay more for them, but you can choose exactly what you want (for a sampling, see the photo above).

Countertops

THINK STYLE, DURABILITY, AND EASY MAINTENANCE

Chop on it, knead on it, serve from it: you ask a lot, every day, of your kitchen countertop. No one material is best for all purposes, but each of those described below and on the facing page looks distinctive and has specific merits.

What are the choices?

Plastic laminate, ceramic tile, solid-surface acrylics, wood, stainless steel, and stone are the six major countertop materials in current use. We discuss each of these options here. Cast concrete and soapstone are both showing up, too—most often in modernistic and traditional designs, respectively.

Shopping around

The problem is that you probably won't find all these materials in the same place. Some dealers are listed in the yellow pages under Countertops or Kitchen Cabinets & Equipment; they'll probably have tile, plastic laminate, solid-surface products, and—maybe—wood. Large home centers and lumberyards usually carry plastic laminate and wood. For other dealers or fabricators, check listings under Concrete Products, Marble—Natural, Plastics, Restaurant Equipment, Sheet Metal Work, and Tile. Designers and architects can also supply samples of materials.

COMPARING COUNTERTOPS

Plastic laminate

Advantages. You can choose from a wide range of colors, textures, and patterns. Laminate is durable, easy to clean, water resistant, and relatively inexpensive. Ready-made molded versions are called post-formed; custom or self-rimmed countertops are built from scratch atop particleboard or plywood substrates. There are many more laminates available for the latter tops, and edging options abound. With the right tools, you can install laminate yourself.

Disadvantages. It can scratch, chip, and burn, and it's hard to repair. Ready-made postformed tops can look cheap; other edgings may collect water and grime. Conventional laminate has a dark backing that shows at its seams; new solid-color laminates, designed to avoid this, are more expensive and somewhat brittle. High-gloss laminates show every smudge.

Ceramic tile

Advantages. It's good-looking and comes in many colors, textures, and patterns. It is heat resistant and, if installed correctly, water resistant. Price depends on how many tiles are used and whether they're formed by machine or by hand. Buy a tile that's rated for countertop use. Grout is also available in numerous colors. Patient do-it-yourselfers are likely to have good results.

Disadvantages. Some tile glazes can react adversely to foods, acids, or household chemicals; be sure to ask. Unglazed tiles can be sealed, but some sealers are unsafe around food. Many people find it hard to keep grout satisfactorily clean (using epoxy grout and thin, uniform grout spaces can help). The hard, irregular surface can chip china and glassware.

COMPARING COUNTERTOPS

Solid-surface

Advantages. Durable, water resistant, heat resistant, nonporous, and easy to clean, this marble-like material can be shaped and joined with virtually invisible seams. Many different edge treatments are possible. It allows for a variety of sink installations, including integral units like the one shown on page 89. Blemishes and scratches can be sanded out.

Disadvantages. It's expensive, requiring professional fabrication and installation for best results. It also requires very firm support below. Until recently, color selection was limited to white, beige, and almond; now stone patterns and pastels are common. Costs climb quickly for wood inlays and other fancy edge details.

Wood

Advantages. Wood is handsome, natural, easily installed, and easy on glassware. If given a good surface finish, it can resist water damage. Maple butcher-block, the most popular, is moderately priced; it's sold in 24-, 30-, and 36-inch widths and with either long, edge-grain strips or blockish, end-grain squares. Other hardwoods are sometimes used in wider, edge-joined form.

Disadvantages. It's harder to keep clean than nonporous materials. It can scorch and scratch, and it may blacken or discolor when near a source of moisture. You can seal it with traditional mineral oil or with a longer-lasting, nontoxic penetrating sealer (though cutting might mar this finish). Or use a permanent surface finish, such as polyurethane (but then you definitely can't cut on it).

Stainless steel

Advantages. Stainless steel is waterproof, heat resistant, easy to clean (if matte-finish), and durable. You can get a counter with a sink molded right in. It's great for a part of the kitchen where you'll be using water a lot.

Disadvantages. Don't cut on it, or you risk damaging both countertop and knife. While 16-gauge stainless itself is inexpensive, the cost of fabrication—sink cutouts, faucet holes, and bends and welds for edges and backsplashes—can be quite high. Custom detailing and high-chromium stainless up the price even more. You can, however, reduce the cost by using flat sheeting and a wood edge, as shown at left.

Stone

Advantages. Granite, marble, and limestone all popular for countertops, are beautiful natural materials. Their cool surface is very useful when you're working with dough or making candy. They're heat-proof, water resistant, easy to clean, and very durable.

Disadvantages. Oil, alcohol, and any acid (such as that from lemons or wine) will stain marble and limestone or damage their finish; granite can stand up to all of these. Solid slabs are very expensive, and decorative details add more cost. Recently, some homeowners and designers have turned to stone tiles—including slate—as less expensive alternatives. When considering a stone other than granite, be sure to study the latest sealers.

Waterworks

SINKS, FAUCETS, FILTERS, AND ACCESSORIES ABOUND

The cleanup center sees lots of active duty in every busy kitchen; in fact, studies claim that up to 50 percent of kitchen time is spent there. So doesn't it make sense to pay special attention to sinks, faucets, dishwashers, and related accessories when you're planning your new kitchen?

The new world of sinks

Recently, sinks and faucets have become prime design accents—a place to add a bit of dash to an otherwise restrained scheme.

When it comes to the primary kitchen sink, the traditional single-bowl version has some serious competition. Today's sink is a multitask center, and double-, even triple-bowl designs are now the norm. They come detailed with many custom-fitted accessories, such as cutting boards, colanders, rinsing baskets, and dish racks.

The one exception is the so-called apron sink, an unabashedly old-fashioned single sink that sits atop a lowered base cabinet (one is shown above right).

MATERIALS. Common sink materials include stainless steel, enameled cast iron or steel, composites, and solid-surface acrylics. Vitreous china is also making a comeback. For smaller auxiliary sinks or "bar" sinks, you can use more decorative surfaces like copper or brass. All of these materials are outlined on the facing page.

In addition, you may see new sinks made from ceramic fireclay, concrete, or soapstone. Color-consistent fireclay seems especially promising, since scratches or dings can be scrubbed or buffed out.

SINK SIZES. The traditional one-piece sink measures about 22 inches deep and 24 inches wide. Double- or one-and-a-half-bowl sinks average 33 inches wide; triple-bowl versions, or those with integral drain boards, can stretch to 42 inches. Sinks are getting deeper, a boon for those washing big pots and baking sheets.

RIM OR NO RIM? You also have a choice of mounting methods with vari-

A country kitchen's apron sink sits atop a lowered base cabinet. They're joined by an old-fashioned wall faucet and a pine-paneled dishwasher.

ous sink models. Self-rimming sinks with molded overlaps are supported by the edge of the countertop cutout; they work well with any countertop material. Undermounted sinks are positioned under the countertop and held in place by metal clips; they have a modern look that works well with stone and solid-surface edges. Flush-mounted sinks are set into the counter substrate to align with the surface material—usually tile.

COMPARING SINKS

Stainless steel

Stainless steel sinks come in 18- to 22-gauge (18-gauge is best, 22-gauge is flimsy) and either matte or mirror finish. Chromium/nickel blends are the only true "stainless" sinks; cheaper grades will stain. Matte finishes are much easier to keep looking clean than mirrored, and they mask scratches better. You'll find a large selection of double- and triple-bowl designs; integral drain boards are available, too. Stainless is relatively noisy, so look for a sink with an undercoating.

Enameled cast iron/steel

Here's where the colors come in. Enameled cast-iron sinks have a heavier layer of baked-on enamel than steel, making them quieter and less likely to chip, but also more expensive. These sinks have become quite popular, especially with the advent of new European designs. White, black, gray, and a palette of other colors and flecked patterns are available in many double- and triple-bowl models. The cast edges of self-rimming versions are prone to warping; be sure to check when you take delivery.

Composite

This durable, resilient newcomer comes with either a smooth or textured finish; it's lighter than cast iron. Composite can be fairly expensive. Some complain about limited style and color options (usually white or off-whites); some dislike the "plastic" look. Quartz sinks, or composites with high quartz content, are toughest; they resemble enamel but are easier to maintain.

Integral solid-surface

Today's solid-surface countertop (see page 87) can be coupled with a molded, integral sink for a sleek, sculpted look. Sink color can either match the counter-top exactly or complement it. Edge-banding and other border options abound, including decorative grooving and adjacent drain boards. Although they're not indestructible, solid-surface sinks can be repaired if nicked or scratched. These sinks come in single-bowl versions only. Check the depth—they may not be as deep as you'd like.

Vitreous china

Vitreous china sinks, a common bathroom component, are starting to show up in the kitchen. The material (made with clay that's poured into molds, fired in a kiln, and glazed) is heavy and is easy to clean; it also resists scratches and stains. These are highly ornamental, sculpted sinks, often with handpainted accents. On the down side, they can be very expensive and are subject to chipping.

Brass and copper

These elegant surfaces are outstanding as accents. However, they require considerable maintenance—especially if highly polished—so you may wish to reserve them for wet-bar or other occasional uses. Bar or hospitality sinks come with either a 2- or 3½-inch drain opening; if you're planning to add a disposal (see page 91) you'll want the larger opening. An 18-inch diameter is typical.

Sink faucets run a gamut from old-fashioned to high-tech, from soft pewter-finish to jazzy epoxy, and from single-lever to spread-fit.

Faucets

Today's kitchen faucets fall into one of two camps: European-style or traditional. Enameled single-lever fixtures with pullout sprayers and interchangeable attachments are fashionable, but traditional gooseneck styles with individual handles remain popular, too.

Finishes include polished chrome, brushed chrome, nickel, polished and antiqued brass, soft pewter, elegant gold, and jazzy enameled epoxy. For sheer durability and low maintenance, a polished chrome surface with high nickel content is still the best bet.

Sink faucets are available with single, center-set, or spread-fit controls. A single-lever fitting has a combined faucet and lever or knob controlling water flow and temperature. A center-set control has separate hot and cold water controls and a faucet, all mounted on a base or escutcheon. A spread-fit control has separate hot and cold water controls and a faucet, independently mounted. While most faucets are sink-mounted, certain installations call for either deck-mounted or wall-mounted fittings. When you select your sink, be sure the holes in it will accept the type of faucet you plan to buy as well as any additional accessories, such as hot water dispenser, soap dispenser, water purifier, and a dishwasher's air gap.

Ask yourself three questions when you're attracted to clever, streamlined designs. How well could you work the controls with greasy hands? Can the spout fit over a large pan? And how easy would it be to clean or maintain the installation?

Whatever style you choose, you get pretty much what you pay for. Solid-brass workings, though pricey, are most durable. Ceramic- or plastic-disk valve designs are easier to maintain than older washer schemes.

If you'd like to give yourself a little treat, take a cue from restaurant kitchens. Instead of lugging heavy pots of water from sink to stovetop, consider installing a so-called pot filler (like the one shown at bottom left on the facing page) near the range or cooktop.

Hot & cold water dispensers

Half-gallon-capacity instant hot water dispensers have been around for some time now. The heater fits underneath the sink; connected to the cold water supply, it delivers 190°F to 200°F water. Most units plug into a 120-volt grounded outlet installed inside the sink cabinet. Mount the dispenser either on a sink knockout or nearby on the countertop.

Cold water spouts operate in a similar manner, but a below-counter chiller is substituted for the heater. Some units combine both hot and cold water levers in one unit.

New compact water purifiers look just like hot water or soap dispensers on the sink; the main unit fits compactly below the sink like other water appliances. Filtration systems vary widely. Reverse-osmosis filters are considered most effective, but their output is limited. If you have questions about your water's composition, first have it tested, then choose the right system for the job.

Garbage disposals

Today's garbage disposals handle almost all types of food waste. They come in two types: batch-feed and continuous. Batch-feed disposals kick into gear when you engage the lid; continuous-feed models are activated by an adjacent wall switch or sink-mounted air switch. Batch-feed types are considered safer, but come with fewer options.

Look for sturdy motors (½ horsepower or more), noise insulation, and efficient antijam features. Generally, the fatter the disposal, the more the insulation—and the quieter it's likely to run.

The disposal links with the sink drain below the countertop. It may require its own 120-volt electrical circuit; the connection may be either plug-in or hard-wired.

Some building codes prohibit the use of disposals, while others require them. Be sure to check!

Dishwashers

Whether portable or built-in, most dishwashers are a standard size: roughly 24 inches wide, 24 inches deep, and 34 inches high. A few compact units and European imports come as narrow as 18 inches. Standard finishes include enameled steel (usually white, black, or almond), stainless steel, and black glass. You can also choose replaceable panels to match base cabinet runs.

Quiet is a blessing in a dishwasher—especially when the kitchen is open to adjacent spaces. Improved insulation has led to operating levels as low as 50 decibels.

First, examine the racks. They should be adjustable and able to accommodate your cooking equipment and dishes. Then consider such energy-saving devices as a booster heater that raises the water temperature for the dishwasher only, separate cycles for lightly or heavily soiled dishes, and air-drying choices. Other features include a delay start that allows you to wash dishes at a preset time (during the night instead of at peak-energy hours), prerinse and pot-scrubbing cycles, and a strainer filtering system (actually like a small disposal).

Like a garbage disposal, the dishwasher connects to the sink drain (in fact, it frequently empties directly through the disposal). You'll also need to tap into the hot water supply pipe and provide a separate 120-volt circuit for power. Many local codes require you to install an air gap along with the dishwasher; this device, which mounts atop the sink or countertop, keeps waste water from backing up if there's a drop in water-supply pressure.

POT FILLER

REVERSE-OSMOSIS WATER FILTER

ULTRA-QUIET DISHWASHER

Ranges, Cooktops, and Ovens

GAS OR ELECTRIC, THEY OFFER RED-HOT LOOKS AND EFFICIENCY

What's best, the flexibility of separate cooktops and ovens or the traditional integrated range? On one level, the choice is one of function. But in addition to that, it's a question of style: the range creates a focal point, invoking the traditional image of "hearth and home." Separates, on the other hand, look right in clean, contemporary surroundings.

Ranges

Most ranges have a cooktop with oven below; a few models offer an additional upper microwave oven with a built-in ventilator or downventing cooktop. Standard range width is 30 inches, but sizes go as narrow as 21 inches and, in commercial designs, as wide as 48 inches or more.

FREESTANDING, SLIDE-IN, OR DROP-IN? Take your choice of three range types: freestanding, slide-in, or drop-in. Freestanding ranges sit anywhere; slide-ins are similar, but come without side panels to fit between cabinets. Drop-in models rest on a wood platform within adjacent base cabinets; their integral rims seal any food-collecting gaps.

WHICH STYLE IS FOR YOU? Choose from standard models—gas or electric; reconditioned "heirloom" ranges; dual-fuel designs; shiny commercial units; or safer residential/commercial versions. For a discussion of burner options, see pages 94–95; for oven specifics, turn to pages 96–97.

EUROPEAN "HEIRLOOM" RANGE

■ **ELECTRIC RANGES** may have standard coils, solid-element burners, or a smooth ceramic top, plus radiant-heat or combination convection/radiant ovens.

■ **GAS RANGES** have either radiant-heat or convection ovens; lower ovens may be self-cleaning or continuous-cleaning. Some offer interchangeable cooktop modules.

■ **DUAL-FUEL RANGES** combine the responsiveness of a gas cooktop with the even heating of one or two electric ovens—producing, in theory, the best of both worlds.

■ **HEIRLOOM RANGES** are refurbished oldsters that lend an ambiance of comfortable permanence to both country and period design schemes. They're usually freestanding gas models with few modern amenities; some have integral griddles and/or warming trays. New ranges with an "old" look are also available, but these can be very expensive.

■ **COMMERCIAL GAS UNITS** have been much in demand in recent years—partly due to their increased BTU output and partly because of their look of serious culinary business. Their performance is excellent, but they create many problems for home use: they're not as well-insulated as residential units; they may be too heavy for your floor; they're tough to clean; and they're potentially dangerous for children.

■ **RESIDENTIAL/COMMERCIAL UNITS**, a recent response to the commercial craze, were designed specifically for the home. These have the commercial look and the high BTU output but are better insulated; they also offer additional niceties such as pilotless ignition and self- or continuous-cleaning ovens.

DROP-IN RANGE

RESIDENTIAL/COMMERCIAL RANGE

Cooktops

For flexibility, specialized cooking, or simply a trim, modern look, separate cooktops make good sense. Their rapidly increasing use in island and peninsula designs is part of this trend.

Before confronting the bewildering array of cooktops on the market, you'll need to make some basic decisions. First, what type of energy do you prefer? Gas units heat and cool quickly, and the flame is visible and easy to control. Electric units provide low, even heat. Unless you buy a downventing

MODULAR COOKTOP

COMPARING COOKTOPS

Smoothtop (ceramic glass)

Electric smoothtop cooktops have burners similar to traditional coil designs but with ceramic glass on top, which disperses heat and makes the cooktop much easier to clean. In the past, these tops have received thumbs down for slow heating, but newer designs have coils closer to the surface; some models also include fast-starting coils. Warning lights on some new models stay on until the top is cool enough to touch.

Early smoothtops also scratched or cracked. Newer formulations are more durable. Popular finishes include classic black and flecked patterns (the latter hide abrasions). Look for independent sizing controls for smaller or larger pans. Smoothtop surfaces require flat-bottom pans for best heat dispersal.

Solid-element electric

These trim-looking burner units are basically cast-iron disks with resistance coils below. Because of the continuous surface, the disks produce more even heat than standard coils; and because they're sealed, they're easier to clean. Better models have thermostats or on-off cycles to keep heat even and to protect the unit. With some, central "button" sections glow when the power is on.

Owner complaints? Solid-element burners may not produce enough heat for certain types of cooking. The disks may discolor over time with overzealous scrubbing. Like smoothtop surfaces, solid-element disks require flat-bottom pans for best results.

Induction

This is cooking with magnetism, and the response is as instant as gas. Once you set an appropriate pan in place and turn on the unit, a sensor triggers an induction coil that sets up an electromagnetic field reaching about an inch above the cooking surface. Remove the pan and there's no live heat source. Chefs love induction's ability to slow-simmer.

Are there minuses? Induction is expensive and not widely available. You must use pans of a ferrous metal—cast iron, magnetic stainless steel, or porcelain steel. Some cooks complain that it won't produce enough heat.

model, the cooktop will require an overhead hood. (For venting specifics, see pages 98–99).

■ **STANDARD** gas and electric cooktops are built into counters like self-rimming sinks, with connections below. Most units have four burners, though some have five, six, or even more. The majority of cooktops come in 30- or 36-inch widths; they're all at least 2 to 3 inches shallower than the standard 24-inch cabinet depth. Drop-in cooktops with no venting included run from about 2½ to 8 inch-

es high; figure about 16½ inches for downventing models.

■ **CONVERTIBLE** gas and electric cooktops are similar to conventional models but offer interchangeable and reversible modules that let you replace burners with grills, griddles, and other specialized accessories.

■ **COMMERCIAL** or residential/ commercial (see page 93) gas units house up to eight burners; many styles offer hot plates or griddles. Typically, burners are 6 to 7 inches high with short legs for installing on a base of tile, brick, or

other noncombustible material.

■ **MIX-AND-MATCH MODULES** or "hobs," typically 12 inches wide, may be grouped together with connecting hardware or embedded separately, if you choose. Modules consist of standard gas, halogen, smoothtop electric, solid-element electric, barbecue, griddle, electric wok, or deep fryer (sometimes also serving as steamer) units. Some of these fit in as little as 2 inches of vertical space, freeing up the cabinet below for drawers or a complementary oven.

COMPARING COOKTOPS

Halogen

The latest technological kitchen marvel, halogen rivals magnetic induction as the most "now" of heat sources. Still more expensive to operate than gas, halogen is nonetheless the most efficient electric source; and, unlike most electric burners, halogen offers rapid on-off and infinite adjustment controls.

Halogen burners come as one of a pair of burners in 12-inch modules, or in standard four-burner setups combining one halogen with three standard smoothtop burners. Halogen's weakness? It's still quite expensive. The light can burn out, but is expected to last approximately eight years before needing replacement.

Gas

Gas cooktops are the choice of most gourmet cooks; they respond instantly when turned on or off, or when settings are changed. Gas is also more economical to operate than any electric alternative. Smaller modular units house two standard burners, or one standard (8,000 BTU) and one "commercial" (12,000 BTU). Stylish sealed gas burners are fused to the cooktop; they're easier to clean than conventional burners and just as efficient. All standard units have pilotless ignition now, and some manufacturers offer an instant reignition feature.

Drawbacks? Some people dislike the odor. Gas may be harder to maintain than an electrical heat source. Simmering can be difficult. White grates may discolor over time.

Commercial gas

Commercial gas units are made of heavy-duty cast iron or fabricated metal finished in stainless steel, black enamel, or silver gray. Commercial gas cooktops are usually 6 to 7 inches high with short legs for installing on a base of tile, brick, or other noncombustible material. They often come with hot plates or griddles. Simmering can be difficult; a cast-iron simmer top may be available.

Commercial/residential gas units combine the commercial output with features such as integral top grates, designer colors, and self-insulation (so installing requires no additional insulation).

Wall ovens

Built-in ovens save counter space by fitting inside base cabinets or special vertical storage units. With separate ovens, as with cooktops, you have several choices: conventional radiant heat, convection, or microwave.

Teaming a conventional oven with a microwave or energy-saving convection oven is a popular choice. Double ovens can be installed one above the other or side by side below the countertop (some cooks find this a convenient use of space, while others find it frustrating). You can also purchase combination or multi-mode units that allow you to switch between functions, but they're pricey.

Your oven's interior may be "you-clean" (old-fashioned elbow grease required), continuous cleaning (a steady, slow process with a result that may never look clean), or self-cleaning (pyrolytic)—the most effective method.

RADIANT-HEAT OVENS. Conventional radiant-heat ovens are available as single or double units. Built-in ovens are sized to fit standard, 24-inch-deep cabinet cavities; deeper units are also available. The most common width is 27 inches, though many space-efficient European imports are 24 inches; recently, the 30-inch-wide oven has caught on. So-called "built-under" ovens provide a range effect without interrupting the countertop; add the low-clearance cooktop of your choice.

You can choose to include built-in warmer shelves, rotisseries, attached meat thermometers, variable-speed broilers, multiple-rack systems, pizza inserts, and digital timing devices.

STACKED WALL OVENS

WARMING OVENS

CONVECTION OVENS. Both gas and electric convection ovens use a fan to circulate hot air around the oven cavity. More energy-efficient than radiant-heat ovens, they can cut cooking time by 30 percent and use reduced temperatures. So-called "true-convection" models have isolated heating elements and fans to provide more even results.

Convection is excellent for roasting and baking (it first caught on in commercial bakeries) but is less effective for foods cooked in deep or covered dishes (cakes, stews, casseroles). Some cooks complain that convection heat dries out certain foods.

MICROWAVE OVENS. Foods cook quickly with high-frequency microwaves, but they don't brown. Some models offer a separate browning element; other built-ins combine microwave with radiant and/or convection cooking. Microwave models range from subcompacts (about .5 cubic foot) up to full size (1 cubic foot or bigger). Most units are hinged on the left.

BUILT-UNDER OVEN

OVER-COUNTER MICROWAVE

Microwaves can be placed on a counter, built into cabinetry, or purchased as part of a double wall oven or double oven range. You might even consider two microwaves—one small, portable unit near the refrigerator or breakfast nook for quick warming, the second in a bank of wall ovens. When possible, mount the microwave so its bottom is 24 to 48 inches off the floor.

Some models, specially designed to be installed above a range (underneath wall cabinets), incorporate a vent and cooking lights; these are wider (30 inches) and shallower (13 to 17 inches deep). Some designers frown on over-the-cooktop placement because it's potentially hazardous when burners below are in use.

Microwave features include memory bank, programmable cooking, timers, temperature probe, rotisserie, and electronic sensors (these automatically calculate cooking time and power levels). However, if you use a microwave primarily to heat coffee or convenience foods, you can probably bypass these bells and whistles.

Ventilation

CLEAN THE AIR—AND DO IT WITH STYLE

Installing a kitchen without planning for proper ventilation is akin to lighting a fire in the fireplace without opening the flue. The system you choose must tackle smoke, heat, grease, moisture, and odors, while remaining as quiet as possible (8 sones or less). Vent units range from totally discreet to bold and flashy.

Your main choice is between hoods and downdraft systems.

Vent hoods

Unless your range is downvented, you'll need a hood above the cooktop. Ducted hoods channel air outside; roof- or wall-mounted exterior blowers are the best blend of quiet operation and efficiency. There are two basic types: freestanding and cabinet- or wall-mounted. In addition, the cabinet-mounted hood comes in a sleek, low-profile version that pulls out from under a wall-hung cabinet for use. Whichever type you prefer, look beyond style for convenient, variable speed controls and built-in lighting.

If exterior venting is impossible, cabinet-mounted ductless hoods can draw out some smoke and grease through charcoal filters—but they return air and heat to the room.

A hood should cover the entire cooking area and extend 3 to 6 inches over on each side. If the hood is 16 to 21 inches deep, place its bottom edge 24 inches above cooktop. Position a 24-inch-deep hood up to 30 inches away.

FREESTANDING VENT HOOD

CABINET-MOUNTED HOOD

Downdraft systems

If your kitchen style is open and orderly, you may wish to put a downdraft system in the range or cooktop instead of a hood overhead—especially if the unit is housed in an island or peninsula. Standard, convertible, and modular cooktops all come with downventing options. Some have grillwork between cooktop modules; others run along the back and may be raised electronically for use. The downdraft unit sets up air currents that draw smoke, heat, and moisture down; grease is trapped below.

Are there drawbacks? Downvents don't work as well on a tall stockpot as on a skillet at cooktop level. However, recent systems are more efficient than those available just a few years ago. There have also been problems with long, twisted duct runs. Always route a downdraft system to the closest outside wall.

What size do you need?

The power of a fan or blower is rated in cubic feet per minute (CFM).

To find the number of CFM for your wall- or cabinet-mounted hood, the basic formula is: 50 to 70 CFM times the square footage (length times width) of the hood opening. The minimum rating is 300 CFM.

To determine the rating for a freestanding hood, the formula is: 100 CFM times the hood's square footage.

The minimum rating is 600 CFM. The shorter and straighter the duct run, the more efficient your hood will be.

Commercial ranges and cooktops can really crank out the heat; you may need to make extra provisions for these. In addition, if you live in a super-insulated modern house and are planning a powerful vent system, you could require an intake fan or window to replace the air that's being sucked out. If you have questions, consult an experienced HVAC professional.

LOW-PROFILE, PULLOUT HOOD

DOWNDRAFT VENT

Refrigerators

COOL NEW ALTERNATIVES TO THE OLD ICEBOX

BUILT-IN, SIDE-BY-SIDE REFRIGERATOR, OPEN AND CLOSED

Refrigerators come in three basic versions: freestanding, built-in, and under-counter. Which you choose depends on space, aesthetics, and budget. You'll want to take a close look at available features. Think energy, too: every refrigerator should come with an energy guide label that tells you just how that model rates.

Freestanding models

Standard refrigerators measure from 27 to 32 inches deep, so they stand out from 24-inch-deep base cabinets.

Consider these features: number of shelves, humidity drawers, meat storage compartments, temperature controls, defrosting method, ice-maker and water dispenser, convenience

UNDER-COUNTER WINE COOLER

MODULAR PULLOUT DRAWER

door, and energy-saving devices such as a power-saver switch.

Popular two- or three-door, side-by-side refrigerator/freezers permit easy visibility and access to food, but their relatively narrow shelves make it difficult to store bulky items. Their opposing door swings can block countertop access on both sides.

Other double-door models have the freezer positioned at the unit's bottom or top. The bottom-mount design has a handy freezer pullout drawer and makes it easier to reach the more often used refrigerator section. The top-mount style comes in the greatest number of sizes and options.

Though single-door refrigerators are smaller and more economical, they typically offer little freezer space, and that space may not get cold enough. Many of these units must be defrosted manually.

As a rule of thumb, figure 8 cubic feet of refrigerator space for two people; add 1 cubic foot for each additional family member and 2 extra cubic feet if you entertain frequently. A refrigerator runs best when it isn't stuffed to the gills.

Two cubic feet per person is the rule for a freezer compartment.

Built-ins

Gaining in popularity are relatively expensive 24-inch-deep built-ins, which fit right into a standard run of cabinets. Most models offer interchangeable door panels to match surrounding cabinet doors. Others flaunt the "commercial" look, matching stainless steel with glass doors.

Because these units have compressor and condenser units mounted on top, they don't require dust-gathering gaps for ventilation; they also can be

cleaned and serviced in place. One minus (besides the high price) is the relatively shallow interior.

Under-counter models

Standard under-counter refrigerators, traditional choices for very small kitchens or separate entertainment areas, are 33 to 34 inches high, 18 to 57 inches wide, and 25 to 32 inches deep, with a 2.5- to 6-cubic-foot capacity.

Now there's also a new generation of trim built-ins that slide into 24-inch-deep base cabinet runs, offering interchangeable refrigerator, freezer, and even wine-cooling compartments. Some models feature handy pullout drawers for easy low-level access. Not only do these "modular" units blend into sleek modern kitchens, they can be positioned just where they're needed in multitask, several-cook layouts.

Trash Talk

PUT GRIME AND GARBAGE IN THEIR PLACES

Frequently, today's cleanup centers include both a dishwasher (see page 91) and a trash compactor—one on either side of the sink. In addition, you'll find a broad selection of built-in bins, baskets, and pullouts for organizing trash, recyclables, and composting scraps. Here are some shopping tips.

Trash compactors

Compactors reduce bulky trash such as cartons, cans, and bottles to a fourth of the original size. A typical compacted load—a week's worth of trash from a family of four—will weigh 20 to 28 pounds. Remember that a compactor is for dry, clean trash only—you'll still have to do some work.

Once considered an unequivocal boon, the trash compactor is currently viewed with disdain by many. Opponents state that recycling programs in urban areas have made compactors unnecessary; others argue that compressed trash takes longer to break down in landfills. But in remote locales, or in spots where recycling is nonexistent or impractical, a compactor might at least reduce the volume of trash that's thrown away.

If you're considering one, look for such features as a separate top-bin door for loading small items (even while the unit is operating), drop-down or tilt-out drawers for easy bag removal, and a charcoal-activated filter or deodorizer to control odor. Also

RECYCLING BINS

look for a toe-operated door latch and a key-activated safety switch.

Standard appliance colors are available; finish options include custom wood panels with or without trim kits. Sizes vary from 12 to 18 inches wide (15 inches is standard), 18 to 24½ inches deep, and 34 to 36 inches high.

Bins & baskets

Trudging to the garage with every recyclable can or compost scrap can get old quickly. But where in the kitchen can you temporarily store potato peelings, aluminum and tin cans, glass bottles and jars, plastic milk jugs, newspapers, or paper bags?

If you're lucky enough to have a walk-in pantry, you might find space there for standard recycling bins or baskets. Otherwise, base cabinet drawers and pullouts or tall utility cabinets are the place to start.

Some bins and baskets sit behind standard doors; some pivot into place when the door opens; others slide out on pullout guides or from their own stackable frames. You can also buy special-use base cabinets with built-in dividers and tilt-down bins or retrofit standard two-drawer cabinets. Of course, if you're planning custom cabinets, you can also design your own system.

CLOSING THE DOOR ON LAUNDRY

It's a dirty world, and often all that stands between you and the mess outside is your washer and dryer. They usually do their grime fighting in remote (and inconvenient) recesses of the house—a laundry room, garage, or hallway closet. But increasingly, the dynamic duo is being put to work in the handier, more accessible kitchen.

Here the goal is to hide both machines behind seamless doors when not in use. A standard, side-by-side pair can be housed in a recessed alcove or a popout that borrows from an adjacent space. Add shelves or wall cabinets for laundry goods, and perhaps a utility sink alongside. Cover it all up with easy-to-open bifold, sliding, or pocket doors—or with seamless cabinet doors that offer access to each area independently.

Or nestle a compact washer and dryer—either side-by-sides or stackables—into a continuous cabinet run, masking them with standard cabinet doors to match surroundings. Adjacent cabinets or drawers might house an ironing board, a pullout sorting table, and a tilt-down clothes bin.

Remember that you'll need to wire and plumb these appliances as required; also, a gas dryer will require a vent duct to the outside.

A stackable washer and dryer (top left) saves floor space; a built-in ironing board (top right) folds behind its closed door. Side-by-side unit (above) slides below counter height.

Flooring

ADD A FIRM—OR EVEN A RESILIENT—FOUNDATION

Two primary requirements for a kitchen floor are moisture resistance and durability. Resilient flooring, ceramic tile, and properly sealed hardwood or masonry are all good candidates. Resilient flooring is the simplest (and usually the least expensive) of the four to install; the other three are trickier. Tinted concrete is also catching on in high-tech surroundings. And don't rule out carpeting, especially the newer stain-resistant industrial versions.

Planning checkpoints

Confused by the array of flooring types available today? For help, study the guide on the facing page. It's also a good idea to visit flooring suppliers and home centers; most dealers are happy to provide samples.

Beyond aesthetic considerations, you need to weigh the physical characteristics of flooring materials. Kitchen floors take a lot of wear and tear. Is your choice water resistant, durable, and easy to maintain? Is it hard to walk on, noisy, or slippery?

What about subflooring?

Don't make any final flooring decision until you know the kind of subfloor your new flooring will require.

With proper preparation, a concrete slab can serve as a base for almost any type of flooring. Other subfloors are more flexible and not suitable for rigid

Cork tiles make a cushy kitchen floor that blends with many styles.

materials such as masonry and ceramic tile unless they are built up with extra underlayment or floor framing. But too many layers underfoot can make the new kitchen floor awkwardly higher than surrounding rooms. If in doubt, check with a building professional or a flooring dealer.

COMPARING FLOORS

Resilient

Advantages. Generally made from solid vinyl or polyurethane, resilients are flexible, moisture and stain resistant, easy to install, and simple to maintain. Another advantage is the seemingly endless variety of colors, textures, patterns, and styles available. Tiles can be mixed to form custom patterns or provide color accents. Old-fashioned linoleum and cork are back as premium-grade materials.

Sheets run up to 12 feet wide, eliminating the need for seaming in many kitchens; tiles are

generally 12 inches square. Vinyl and rubber are comfortable to walk on. Prices are generally modest, but you'll pay more for custom tiles or imported products. A polyurethane finish may eliminate the need for waxing.

Disadvantages. Resilients are relatively soft, making them vulnerable to dents and tears, though such damage can often be repaired. Tiles may collect moisture between seams if improperly installed. Some vinyl still comes with a photographically applied pattern, but most is inlaid; the latter is more expensive but wears much better.

Ceramic tile

Advantages. Made from hard-fired slabs of clay, ceramic tile is available in hundreds of patterns, colors, shapes, and finishes. Its durability and easy upkeep are definite advantages.

Tiles are usually classified as *quarry tile,* commonly unglazed (unfinished) red-clay tiles that are rough and water resistant; *terra-cotta,* unglazed tiles in earth-tone shades; *porcelain pavers,* rugged tiles in stone-like shades and textures; and *glazed floor tile,* available in glossy, matte, or textured finishes and in many colors.

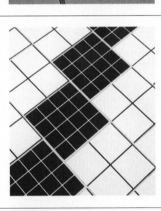

Floor tiles run the gamut of widths, lengths, and thicknesses—8-inch and 12-inch squares are most plentiful. Costs range from inexpensive to moderate; in general, porcelain is most expensive. Purer clays fired at higher temperature are generally costlier but better wearing.

Disadvantages. Tile can be cold, noisy, and, if glazed, slippery underfoot. Porous tiles will stain and harbor bacteria unless properly sealed. Grout spaces can be tough to keep clean, though mildew-resistant or epoxy grout definitely helps.

Hardwood

Advantages. A classic hardwood floor creates a warm decor, feels good underfoot, and can be refinished. Oak is most common, with maple, birch, and other species also available.

The three basic types are narrow *strips* in random lengths; *planks* in various widths and random lengths; and wood *tiles,* laid in blocks or squares. Wood flooring may be factory-prefinished or unfinished, to be sanded and finished in place. "Floating" floor systems have several veneered strips atop each backing board. In

addition, you'll now find "planks" and "tiles" of high-pressure plastic laminate that look surprisingly like the real thing.

Disadvantages. Moisture damage and inadequate floor substructure are two bugaboos. Maintenance is another issue; some surfaces can be mopped or waxed, some cannot. Bleaching and some staining processes may wear unevenly and are difficult to repair. Cost is moderate to high, depending on wood species, grade, and finish.

Stone

Advantages. Natural stone (such as slate, flagstone, marble, granite, and limestone) has been used as flooring for centuries. Today, its use is even more practical, thanks to the development of efficient sealers and surfacing techniques. Stone can be used in its natural shape—known as flagstone—or cut into rectangular blocks or more formal tiles. Generally, pieces are butted tightly together; irregular flagstones require wider grout joints.

Disadvantages. The cost of masonry flooring can be quite high, though recent diamond-saw technology has lowered it considerably. Moreover, the weight of the materials requires a very strong, well-supported subfloor. Some stone is cold and slippery underfoot, though new honed and etched surfaces are safer, subtler alternatives to polished surfaces. Certain stones, such as marble and limestone, absorb stains and dirt readily. Careful sealing is a must.

Windows and Skylights

HELP YOUR NEW DESIGN SEE THE LIGHT OF DAY

Whether you'd like a sunny breakfast nook, a greenhouse unit for culinary plants, or simply a row of glass block sparkling in a backsplash area, you have an impressive collection of both ready-made and custom products to choose from. You can also combine glass in different forms (windows, skylights, blocks) and finishes (clear, translucent) to bring in more light and view while still protecting privacy.

Windows

Windows are available with frames made of wood, clad wood, aluminum, vinyl, steel, or fiberglass (a newcomer). Generally, aluminum windows are the least expensive, wood and clad wood the most costly. Vinyl- or aluminum-clad wood windows and all-vinyl windows require little maintenance.

Operable windows for kitchens include double-hung, casement, sliding, hopper, and awning types. Which you choose depends partly on your home's style and partly on your ventilation needs. In addition, there are such specialty units as bays and bows—both popular for "stretching" breakfast areas—and greenhouse units, which can add space behind the sink or countertop.

Many of the greatest strides in window technology are taking place in glazing. Insulating glass is made of two or more panes of glass sealed together, with a space between the

panes to trap air. Low-e (low-emissivity) glass usually consists of two sealed panes separated by an air space and a transparent coating. Some manufacturers use argon gas between panes of low-e glass to add extra insulation.

Window shopping can require at least a passing acquaintance with

Among the myriad of window styles are (1) primed wood casement with simulated divided lights, (2) wood slider with aluminum cladding and snap-on grille, (3) prefinished wood casement, (4) anodized aluminum slider, (5) vinyl double-hung, (6) wood circle with aluminum cladding, and (7) aluminum octagon.

some specialized jargon. For a quick gloss, see "Window Words," at right.

Skylights

You can pay as little as $100 for a fixed acrylic skylight, about $500 for a pivoting model that you crank open with a pole, or several thousand dollars for a motorized unit that automatically closes when a moisture sensor detects rain. The most energy-efficient designs feature double glazing and "thermal-break" construction.

Fixed skylights vary in shape from square to circular; they may be flat, domed, or pyramidal in profile. Most skylight manufacturers also offer at least one or two ventilating models that open to allow fresh air in and steam and heat out. Think of rotary roof windows as a cross between windows and skylights. They have sashes that rotate on pivots on each side of the frame, which permits easy cleaning. Unlike openable roof skylights, they are typically installed on sloping walls.

If there's space between the ceiling and roof,

WINDOW WORDS

Strange, intimidating words seem to orbit the subject of windows and their components, construction, and installation. Here's a crash course in standard window jargon, enough to help you brave a showroom, building center, or product brochure.

Apron. An applied interior trim piece that runs beneath the unit, below the sill.

Casement. A window with a frame that hinges on the side, like a door.

Casing. Wooden window trim, especially interior, added by owner or contractor. Head casing runs at the top, side casings flank the unit.

Cladding. A protective sheath of aluminum or vinyl covering a window's exterior wood surfaces.

Flashing. Thin sheets, usually metal, that protect the wall or roof from leaks near the edges of windows or skylights.

Glazing. The window pane itself—glass, acrylic plastic, or other clear or translucent material. It may be one, two, or even three layers thick.

Grille. A decorative, removable grating that makes an expanse of glass look as though it were made up of many smaller panes.

Jamb. The frame that surrounds the sash or glazing. An extension jamb thickens a window to match a thick wall.

Lights. Separately framed panes of glass in a multipane window; each light is held by muntins.

Low emissivity. A high-tech treatment that sharply improves the thermal performance of glass, especially in double-glazed windows, at little added cost.

Mullion. A vertical dividing piece; whereas muntins separate small panes of glass, mullions separate larger expanses or whole windows.

Muntin. A slender strip of wood or metal framing a pane of glass in a multipane window.

R-value. Measure of a material's ability to insulate; the higher the number, the lower your heating or cooling bills should be.

Sash. A window frame surrounding glass. It may be fixed or operable.

Sill. An interior or exterior shelf below a window unit. An interior sill may be called a stool.

U-value. Measure of the energy efficiency of all the materials in the window; the lower the U-value, the less the waste.

GLASS BLOCK

you'll need a light shaft to direct light to the room below. It may be straight, angled, or splayed (wider at the bottom).

Glass block

If you'd like to have some ambient daylight but don't want to lose your privacy, check out another glazing option, glass block. It provides an even, filtered light that complements many kitchen designs.

You can buy 3- or 4-inch-thick glass blocks in many sizes; rectangular and curved corner blocks are also available in a more limited selection. Textures can be smooth, wavy, rippled, bubbly, or crosshatched. Some blocks are clear, others softly translucent.

To locate glass block, look in the yellow pages under Glass—Block Structural, Etc. You may be able to special-order blocks through a regular glass or tile dealer.

Light Fixtures

SPOTLIGHTING THE LATEST IN ARTIFICIAL LIGHT SOURCES

WALL SCONCES

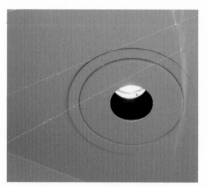

RECESSED DOWNLIGHT

TRACK FIXTURES

LOW-VOLTAGE CABLE LIGHT

UNDER-CABINET STRIP LIGHTS

Designers separate lighting into three categories: task, ambient, and accent. Task lighting illuminates a particular area where a visual activity—such as measuring baking ingredients—takes place. Ambient, or general, lighting fills in the undefined areas of a room with a soft level of light—enough, say, to munch a midnight snack by. Accent lighting, which is primarily decorative, is used to highlight architectural features, to set a mood, or to provide drama.

Which fixtures are best?

Generally speaking, small and discreet are the bywords in kitchen light fixtures; consequently, recessed downlights are the most popular choice in today's kitchens. Though these fixtures, fitted with the right baffles or shields, can handle ambient, task, and accent needs by themselves, you'll probably want other sources, too, at least to fill in shadows. Typically, downlights follow countertops or shine on the sink or island. Track lights or mono-spots also offer pinpoint task lighting and can be aimed at a wall to provide a wash of ambient light.

In addition, designers frequently tuck task lighting behind a valance under wall cabinets and over countertops. For a whimsical touch, you might run decorative strip lights in a toe-space area or soffit.

Surface-mounted fixtures, once a kitchen mainstay, are now used specifically to draw attention. Hanging pendants are attractive in a breakfast nook or over an island—or anywhere where they won't present a hazard. Low-voltage cable lights combine the flexibility of standard track fixtures with a dash of high-tech style.

Dimmers (also called rheostats) enable you to set a fixture at any level from a soft glow to a radiant brightness. They also save energy.

Light bulbs and tubes

Light sources can be grouped according to the way they produce light. INCANDESCENT LIGHT. This light, the kind used most frequently in our homes, is produced by a tungsten thread that burns slowly inside a glass bulb. A-bulbs are the old standbys; R- and PAR- bulbs produce a more controlled beam; and silvered-bowl types diffuse light. A number of decorative bulbs are also available.

Low-voltage incandescent lighting is especially useful for accent lighting. Operating on 12 or 24 volts, these lights require transformers, which are sometimes built into the fixtures, to step down the voltage from 120-volt household circuits.

Low-voltage fixtures are relatively expensive to buy. But in the long run, low-voltage lighting can be energy- and cost-efficient if carefully planned.

FLUORESCENT LIGHT.

Fluorescent tubes are unrivaled for energy efficiency and last far longer than incandescent bulbs. In some areas, general lighting for new kitchens must be fluorescent.

Older fluorescent tubes have been criticized for noise, flicker, and poor color rendition. Electronic ballasts and better fixture shielding have remedied the first two problems; as for the last one, manufacturers have developed fluorescents in a wide spectrum of colors, from very warm to very cool.

QUARTZ HALOGEN.

These bright, white sources are excellent for task lighting, pinpoint accenting, and other dramatic accents. Halogen is usually low-voltage but may use standard line current. The popular MR-16 bulb creates the tightest beam; for a longer reach and wider coverage, choose a PAR-bulb.

Halogen has two disadvantages: its high initial cost and its very high heat production. Be sure to choose a fixture specifically intended for halogen bulbs, and shop for UL-approved fixtures.

COMPARING LIGHT BULBS AND TUBES

INCANDESCENT

A-Bulb	**Description.** Familiar pear shape; frosted or clear. **Uses.** Everyday household use.
T—Tubular	**Description.** Tube-shaped, from 5" long. Frosted or clear. **Uses.** Cabinets, decorative fixtures.
R—Reflector	**Description.** White or silvered coating directs light out end of funnel-shaped bulb. **Uses.** Directional fixtures; focuses light where needed.
PAR—Parabolic aluminized reflector	**Description.** Similar to auto headlamps; special shape and coating project light and control beam. **Uses.** Recessed downlights and track fixtures.
Silvered bowl	**Description.** A-bulb, with silvered cap to cut glare and produce indirect light. **Uses.** Track fixtures and pendants.
Low-voltage strip	**Description.** Like Christmas tree lights; in strips or tracks, or encased in flexible, waterproof plastic. **Uses.** Task lighting and decoration.

FLUORESCENT

Tube	**Description.** Tube-shaped, 5" to 96" long. Needs special fixture and ballast. **Uses.** Shadowless work light; also indirect lighting.
PL—Compact tube	**Description.** U-shaped with base; 5¼" to 7½" long. **Uses.** In recessed downlights; some PL tubes include ballasts to replace A-bulbs.

QUARTZ HALOGEN

High intensity	**Description.** Small, clear bulb with consistently high light output; used in halogen fixtures only. **Uses.** Specialized task lamps, torchères, and pendants.
Low-voltage MR-16— (mini-reflector)	**Description.** Tiny (2"-diameter) projector bulb; gives small circle of light from a distance. **Uses.** Low-voltage track fixtures, mono-spots, and recessed downlights.
Low-voltage PAR	**Description.** Similar to auto headlight; tiny filament, shape, and coating give precise direction. **Uses.** To project a small spot of light a long distance.

design
credits

FRONT MATTER

1. Design: Brad Polvorosa.
2. Interior designer: Lou Ann Bauer. General contractor: Robert Rosselli. Cabinets: Euro-Art Cabinet/Doug Lucchelli. 4. Interior designer: Susan Christman. Cabinets: Phil Garcia Elements. 5. Kitchen designer: Trish Houck, Kitchen Concepts.

CHAPTER ONE/
A PLANNING PRIMER

6. Architect: Anthony Barnes.
16. The Kitchen Source/The Bath & Beyond. 17. Architect: Backen, Arrigoni & Ross. Cabinetmaker: Werner Schneider Construction. 18. Architect: Lou Kimball. 19. Interior designer: Macfee & Associates Interior Design. 24: Interior designer: Marilyn Riding Design.

CHAPTER TWO/
GREAT KITCHEN IDEAS

26. Architect: Charles Rose. Interior designer: John Schneider. Kitchen designer: Sheron Bailey.

High Style

28.Interior Design: Miller/Stein. 29. Interior designer: Agnes Bourne, Inc. 30 (both): Design: J. Allen Sayles Architecture/Rutt of Lafayette and Tina Chapot. 31 (both). Architect: Remick Associates Architects-Builders, Inc. Interior designer: Donna White Interior Design. 32–33 (all). Design/contractor: City Building, Inc. 34 (both). Interior designer: Kremer Design Group. 35. Architect: Ellen Roche, Mojo Stumer Associates. 36. Interior designer: Ann Carter. 37. Architect: Colleen Mahoney/ Mahoney Architects. General contractor: Cove Contruction. 38. Janice Stone Thomas/Stone•Wood Design, Inc. 39. Janice Stone Thomas/Stone•Wood Design, Inc. 40. Interior designer: Celia Rochford. 41. Architectural and interior designer: Lynn Hollyn. 42. Stove surround, countertops, fireplace: Euro-Stone. Wood island countertop: T.S. Milani. 43. Architect: Kirk Train.

On the Surface

44. Design: Taylor Woodrow. 45. Design: Adele Crawford Painted Finishes. 46.Architect: Miller/Hull. 47. Architects: Dail Dixon and Ellen Weinstein. 48 top. Design: Joan Fulton. 48 bottom. Architect: Dennis DeBiase. 49. Interior designer: Steven W. Sanborn. 50 top. Tile artisan: Rodger Dunham Ceramic Design of Petaluma. 50 bottom. Architect: Lindy Small. Concrete: Concreteworks Studio.

51. Interior designer: Macfee & Associates Interior Design.

Storage Solutions

52.Architect: Alison Wright Architects. 53. Architect: Robert Nebolon. 54. Interior designer: Lou Ann Bauer. Contractor: Robert Rosselli. Cabinets: Euro-Art Cabinet/Doug Lucchelli. 55 top. Stove surround: Euro-Stone. 55 bottom. Interior designer: Kremer Design Group. 56 top. Interior designer: Susan Christman. Cabinets: Phil Garcia Elements. 56 bottom. Design/contractor: City Building, Inc. 57. Interior designer: Steven W. Sanborn. 58 top: Janice Stone Thomas/ Stone• Wood Design, Inc. 58 bottom (both). Architect: Heidi Richardson. 59. Architect: Heather H. McKinney.

Bright Ideas

60. Architect: Colleen Mahoney/ Mahoney Architects. General con-tractor: Cove Contruction. 61. Architect: Robert Nebolon. 62. Architect: Mark Horton. 63. Architect: Marcy Li Wong. 64. Interior designer: Osburn Design. 65. Lighting designer: Melinda Morrison. Lighting design architects: Byron Kuth, Liz Ranieri, Doug Thornley (Kuth/Ranieri). 66. Architect: Marc Randall Robinson. Design: Epifanio Juarez/Juarez Design. Interior Architecture and Design: Scott Design. 67. Interior design and lighting: Margaret M. Wimmer. Architect: Carrasco & Associates.

Elegant Options

68. Architect: Stanley Smith. 69. Interior designer: Lou Ann Bauer. Contractor: Robert Rosselli. Cabinets: Euro-Art Cabinet/Doug Lucchelli. 70 (both). Architect: Mulder/Katkov Architecture. 71. Interior designer: Osburn Design. 72–73 (all). Design: Nancy Cowall Cutler. 74 top. Interior

PHOTOGRAPHERS

Unless noted, all photographs are by Philip Harvey.
Jean Allsopp: 47. Patrick Barta: 48 top. Glenn Christiansen: 87 (stainless). Grey Crawford: 48 bottom, 68 bottom, 103 bottom. Mark Darley: 63, 84 bottom. Delta Faucet Co.: 90 top right. Doug Dun: 17. Chris Eden: 46. General Electric Co.: 91 center, 93 left. Hales: 5, back cover bottom. Paul Harris: 52 bottom. Iron-A-Way, Inc.: 103 top right. Ken Jenkins: 84 top. Jenn-Air Co.: 96 top. KitchenAid, Inc.: 101 left. Kohler Co.: 89 (cast iron), 89 (vitreous). David Duncan Livingston: 19, 28, 51. Sylvia Martin: 6, 18, 40, 43, 59, back cover top. Andrew Mckinney: 72-73 Miele Appliances, Inc.: 97 top, 103 top left. Emily Minton: 36, 68. Norman A. Plate: 50 bottom, 58 bottom left, 58 bottom right, 108 bottom left. Rev-a-Shelf, Inc.: 102. Mark Samu: 35. Sub-Zero Freezer Co.: 100 (both). John Vaughan: 93 right. Russ Widstrand: 87 bottom. Tom Wyatt: 45, 86 bottom, 87 top, 92, 94 bottom left, 94 bottom center, 95 left, 105 (ceramic), 105 (wood).

index

Page numbers in **boldface** refer to photographs